The Checkless Society

Its Cost Implications

For the Firm

RECENT PUBLICATIONS

Bureau of Business and Economic Research

Bank Administered Pooled Equity Funds for Employee Benefit Plans
Frank L. Voorheis

The Performance Post Audit in State Government
Lennis M. Knighton

Passenger Transportation
Stanley C. Hollander

The Effects of Data-Processing Service Bureaus on the Practice of Public Accounting
Constantine Konstans

Work Role Involvement of Industrial Supervisors
John G. Maurer

Selection of New Suppliers by the Mobile Family
James E. Bell, Jr.

The Checkless Society:
Its Cost Implications for the Firm
William H. Mateer

A more complete list of publications appears at the end of this volume.

The Checkless Society

Its Cost Implications For the Firm

WILLIAM H. MATEER

1969

MSU BUSINESS STUDIES
Bureau of Business and Economic Research
Division of Research
Graduate School of Business Administration
Michigan State University, East Lansing

Acknowledgments

This study reflects the combined efforts and support of numerous individuals. Although the nature of their contribution varies widely, each is important in its own way and is greatly appreciated.

My gratitude is especially extended to Professors James Don Edwards, Gardner M. Jones, and Floyd W. Windal of the Graduate School of Business Administration, Michigan State University; Joseph L. Saupe of the University of Missouri, and David A. Drinkwater of Babson Institute; to the owner-president of the company participating in the case study; to the Earhart Foundation; and to my family.

Library of Congress Catalog Card Number 76-627114

Contents

List of Figures

List of Tables

I
Introduction

In recent months there has been increasing interest in the rapidly developing concept of a cashless, checkless society; a concept which poses cost implications for the firm. The mechanism for handling financial exchanges and liquidity requirements of the producing-consuming units of the economy is expected to change radically within the next ten years. If this forecast is accurate, traditional methods for managing cash, accounts receivable, and trade credit would be modified and substantially removed from the immediate control of the firm. They would be assumed by a centralized financial exchange facility administered by the banking system. The facility would sell financial services to the firm on a variable expense basis, thus replacing the firm's time costs and variable costs currently associated with maintaining cash balances and accounts receivable. Trade credit would be converted to bank credit. The economic feasibility of a centralized financial exchange facility is derived from the developing capacities of automated equipment.

Although the exact form of the checkless society is unclear, its advent appears certain. Its impact will be unsettling. Dale Reistad, Director of Automation for the American Bankers Association, has commented that:

> The implications of the checkless society would fill several textbooks. . . . Since computer mechanization will drastically affect every conceivable type of financial transfer in the future, it will also affect the consumer's every

financial move. By definition, it will, therefore, affect almost every financial move in business and in the economy as well.[1]

The purpose of this study is to develop a model for determining the point at which it becomes advisable for the firm to depart from traditional methods of handling financial exchanges and adopt the services of an integrated financial exchange system. This point represents the maximum amount which the firm can pay to the banking system for integrated exchange services without negatively affecting the firm's financial position. Payments below this point will result in economies.

The Nature of the Exchange Function

The financial exchange function is defined in the context of this study as the provision of a facility for the execution of transfers of purchasing power among the producing-consuming units of the economy. In performing exchanges, provision is also made for the timing of exchanges implying the storing of purchasing power or the extension of credit. To be efficient, the resources devoted to the performance of this function must be minimized in relation to the benefits received.

In analyzing the costs and benefits associated with the exchange function, it is important to distinguish between exchange, liquidity, and credit. Exchange is the process of accounting for and facilitating the transfer of economic value or purchasing power among the units. It requires that parties to exchanges have access to each other, identify and verify values being offered for exchange, and actually execute the transfer. The process, itself, requires the consumption of economic value for its accomplishment. It is this value consumption which must be minimized.

Liquidity is the means for facilitating exchanges. By definition, liquidity implies a state of readiness for exchange. Economic resources are presented in a form acceptable for transfer. Current examples of liquid resources are cash and demand deposits. These are economic values which facilitate the processes of access, identification and verification of value, and transferring value.

Credit is an alternative means of facilitating exchange without tangible evidence of economic value such as has been traditionally embodied in cash or demand deposits. Credit is also a form of liquidity. It facilitates exchange through intangible evidence demonstrating future value to be added to the economy. This intangible evidence is simply a trust that the values anticipated or promised will actually materialize. Credit thereby allows exchangers to have access to each other, to identify and verify values through intangible evidence, and to execute transfers through exchanges of this evidence.

The exchange process, then, relates directly to the transferring of purchasing power among units. To facilitate this exchange, liquid resources which embody tangible evidence of economic values already created and awaiting exchange may be used; or intangible values which represent future value to be created may be used. If cash is used, the cost lies mainly in the alternative uses of this value which have been forgone. If future values are used, the costs lie in the evaluation of the future benefits to be received and the risk associated with the fruition of these benefits.

The problem therefore becomes one of allocating to the exchange mechanism the lowest level of cost in relation to the benefits received. The position taken here is that as the level of specialization and technology increases, the exchange mechanism progresses from a traditional liquidity system to one based on credit. Time costs associated with liquid assets are replaced with costs of credit. At the present time, the developing capacity of automated equipment presents the possibility of furthering this transition.

Traditionally, the exchange function has been controlled to a large extent by the individual firm with the banking system acting in an agency capacity. In this situation, each firm maintains within its control certain assets, liabilities, and variable accounts whose function is that of financial exchange. Primary among these accounts are the firm's most liquid assets—cash and marketable securities. Related accounts are trade receivables and payables which serve as buffers to the cash account and allow for deferred exchanges. In essence, the firm creates its own financial exchange facility by allocating certain of its sources of funds to these specific uses. It is therefore the responsibility of each of the several firms to assume the risks of this "banking" function, in addition to those associated with its primary function of manufacturing or retailing, and to manage these activities in such a way as to maximize returns on the invested resources.

Theoretical statements and models leading to the optimal solution to the exchange decision for the firm are abundant. Their common thesis identifies the optimal level of resources devoted to this function as that point where expected costs associated with liquidity and exchanges are minimized in relation to the expected benefits. To determine this level, the approach is to identify the specific functions which must be performed and the related benefits. When identified, the optimal level can be fixed.

An early treatment of this problem was presented by J. M. Keynes in his *General Theory of Employment, Interest, and Money.*[2] He pointed to three reasons for carrying liquid assets. First, they serve as a medium of exchange and thereby facilitate the transactions of the business. Liquid assets bridge the gap between receipts and expenditures and store value in the interim. This is referred to as the transactions demand for liquidity. Second, due to uncertainties of future transactions requirements, some additional liquidity is maintained to meet irregular needs. This is referred to as the precautionary demand for liquidity. Finally, Keynes pointed out that some liquidity could be maintained for purely speculative purposes. By holding it now, values may go up in the future thus providing gains in wealth. If exact information is known concerning these items, then it is possible to specify the amount of liquidity needed to fulfill this function. This is the optimal level.

More recently, a comprehensive inventory approach to the management of liquid assets was presented in a study by J. C. Burton.[3] His representation of the problem expands Keynes theory and enumerates the kinds of costs associated with the various motives for holding liquid assets. These relationships are shown in Figure 1.

The Burton model in Figure 1 identifies bank credit as a principal source of liquidity. Thus, traditional cash balances and bank credit are combined to satisfy the liquidity needs of the firm.

The management of trade credit may be approached in a similar manner. It is also a part of the exchange function. Such credit represents a delay in the execution of a financial exchange. Accompanying it are the time costs associated with capital uses and several items of variable costs such as credit investigation expenses, bad debts, and clerical costs. Again, with exact information concerning these variables, optimal solutions may be determined.

Although the theoretical framework for liquid asset management is well developed, the problem of implementation remains. Even under conditions of certainty, measurement is difficult. This is greatly complicated in the face of uncertainty and the need to establish

Figure 1
DIAGRAM OF LIQUID ASSET PROBLEM

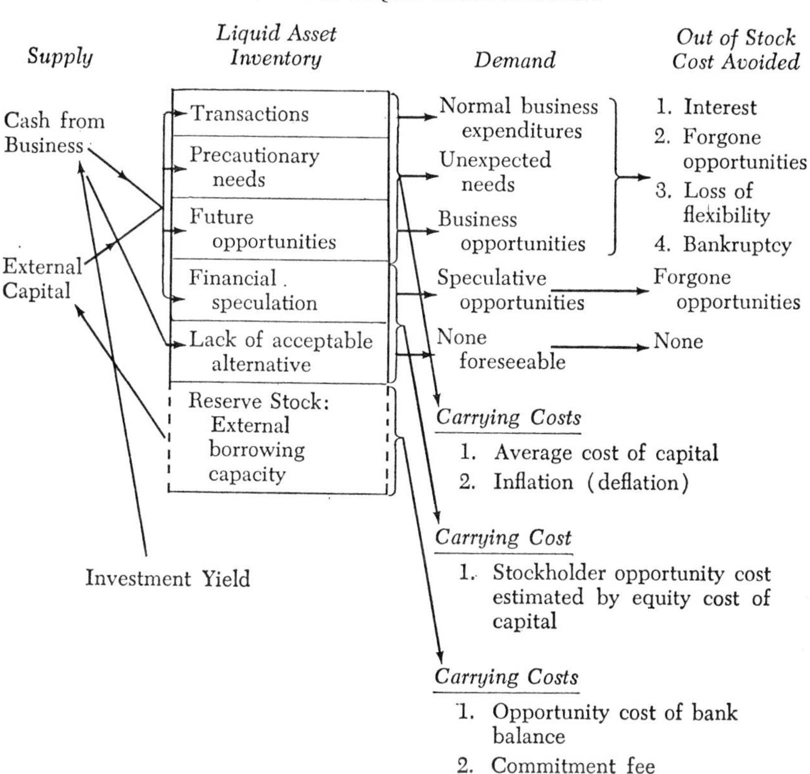

precautionary balances and trade credit needs. As a result, solutions to the problem may vary widely depending upon the size of the firm, the industry changes in demand, attitudes toward risk, and the ability to measure the several variables. The costs of uncertainty and duplication of effort are present.

The concept of a centralized exchange function appears to present the opportunity to gain economies for the firm and the economy. Although the various motives for maintaining the exchange function must remain present, it is thought that its management can be more effective if the banking system's realm of responsibility for the exchange mechanism is increased. Accordingly, risk for the over-capacity or under-capacity of the facility would also be shifted from the firm to the collective system.

In a centralized system, the firm could eliminate its average cash balance, accounts receivable balance, variable exchange and credit expenses, and accounts payable. Exchange needs which these accounts have traditionally fulfilled would now be guaranteed to the firm by the banking system in return for a variable exchange service fee. Any purchase would be recorded automatically reducing the firm's exchange account. The selling firm would receive credit for the sale in its exchange account when the desired service is performed. The exchange account would fluctuate within specified limits with no additional charge or interest payment, provided that an *average* balance of zero was maintained. Should the balance average less than zero resulting from greater outflows than inflows, bank credit would be applied automatically accompanied by an interest fee. If the balance were to average above the zero level, the funds would be invested automatically resulting in interest income.

The exchange service fee is likely to take the form of a percentage discounting of sales. For every sales dollar handled by the banking system, some percentage would be retained as its means of compensation for the service. The rate of the exchange fee would vary from firm to firm depending upon the certainty and pattern of exchange needs. The less certain or regular the needs, the higher the rate charged. Thus, in the centralized system, the firm's exchange needs would be handled entirely by the central banking system. The corporation would come to view operating liquidity as the ability to demonstrate future value added rather than stores of value already created. Purchases of current assets would be accompanied automatically by a fee for facilitating the exchange. As long as the expected value of the purchase materialized, its exchange cost would be covered.

Evidence of the existence of this modified view of liquidity by corporate behavior was presented in a 1965 study, "Corporate Liquidity in the Postwar Period," which reached a conclusion that:

> Both theoretical arguments and examination of institutional factors operative in the postwar period tend to the conclusion that firms will seek primarily to minimize the amounts both of money and its close substitutes that they hold, relative to annual turnover as a measure of "transactions." They are primarily concerned with production or distribution of some commodity or service, to be sold at a profit. One aspect of their productive operations is the generation of a flow of cash from those operations after out-of-pocket costs are met. In a sense, the ability of their productive apparatus to generate cash flows may measure the "liquidity" of their operations, and thus be

George W. Mitchell, a member of the Board of Governors of the Federal Reserve System, has described the advantages of a computerized system for financial exchanges from the banking system's point of view as follows:

> In this system there is no check sorting and re-sorting, no shipment of checks from bank-to-bank or bank-to-customer, no storage requirements for checks, no kited checks, no endorsement, no N. S. F. checks, no float, and a minimum of manual processing. Of course, different problems may later come to light. The machine must work; and the bank must make sure it is being instructed by the owner of the deposit. There is no reason, however, to fear that any such potential difficulties are beyond the technological capacities and probably the cost horizons now in view.[7]

Continuing concerning the efficiency of the total system, Mitchell stated that if his projections are realistic, "they seem to promise, in the aggregate, a substantially more efficient settlement mechanism. And they imply additional profit opportunities for banks that can combine settlement with receivables accounting, payroll accounting, credit card operations, and a consumer credit system for depositors."[8]

A study by the Stanford Research Institute for the Federal Reserve System examines in detail the technical aspects of a computerized payments mechanism from a macro point of view. The report states that "by any standard of measurement, the DFT (Direct Funds Transfer) system offers significant savings over the present system."[9]

Present indications are that such a system is expected to be in limited use by 1975.[10] A part of this study traces the development of actual and expected events leading to the formation of a centralized exchange facility by examining in detail the above three phases of development.

Design and Illustration of the Indifference Point Analysis

While the prospect of a centralized exchange facility as an alternative for handling the firm's exchange needs moves closer to becoming a reality, a method is needed for evaluating its effect on the individual firm. The research thus far published concerning the feasibility of the checkless society is almost exclusively analyzed from the macro viewpoint of the banking system. The question remains as to the extent of savings, if any, to be gained by the individual business.

One opinion survey conducted by the Diebold Group of 2,150

bankers, monetary economists, and financial executives indicated that businesses are likely to be principal beneficiaries of the new exchange mechanism. The following survey question revealed that:

> The principal benefits of an automatic credit and money transfer system will be reaped by:
> a) banks
> b) credit card companies
> c) communications companies
> d) computer equipment manufacturers
> e) credit information businesses
> f) retailers
> g) commercial and industrial enterprises using the system of transactions
> h) the consuming public
>
> Fifty-five percent believe that commercial and industrial enterprises using the automatic system will be among those reaping its principal benefits.[11]

Although such an opinion survey can be very meaningful, the economic implications of the checkless society for the firm remain to be demonstrated quantitatively. To date, figures on benefits and costs for the firm have not been available.

Mitchell states the need for research from the point of view of the firm's costs in the following statement:

> . . . no one really knows how much cost reduction, private and social, a fully computerized system might achieve. . . . One of the difficulties of bringing the relevant evidence together is the problem of totaling up actual private costs in our present settlement system which could be eliminated or reduced in the "checkless-cashless" society.[12]

The method of analysis developed here is designed to provide this type of information for the individual firm.

Present methods for handling the exchange and operating liquidity needs of the firm present a variety of costs. Primary among these are the time costs associated with the carrying of cash balances and accounts receivable. In addition to the time costs, current costs are also incurred such as bank charges, credit investigation expenses, and clerical costs.

The introduction of a centralized exchange function eliminates some of these costs. In their place arises a variable bank charge or bank exchange rate assessed for the handling of all exchange and operating liquidity needs of the firm. To be economically feasible, the new system must present a bank charge which is less than the cost associated with the present system. If there are, in fact, economies to be gained in the performance of the exchange function, then the total cost of the centralized system will be lower than the sum of the individual costs presently being incurred by the several units. At some point, depending upon the bank exchange rate charged, it becomes advisable for the firm to cease performing the exchange function itself and purchase this service from the central system.

It is the determination of this point which is of major concern in this study. To analyze this problem, an indifference point analysis will be applied. The indifference point is defined as the application of that bank exchange rate where the total cost to the firm of the present system for handling financial exchange is equal to the total cost it would incur under the centralized system. This indifference rate indicates the point at which it becomes advisable for the firm to adopt the new system to be offered by the banking system. If the new system can be offered to the firm at less than the indifference bank exchange rate, economies will result.

In its simplest form, the analysis assumes that the costs currently incurred by the firm are limited to those of the cash balance. The cost to the firm is therefore represented by the earning rate required on this use of funds–the cost of capital. Assuming an average cash balance of $15,000, and a cost of capital of 15 percent, after tax earnings must be at least $2,250.

Under the centralized system, three additional variables become relevant. These are sales, the bank exchange rate, and the tax rate. The effective cost under this system is computed as: Sales × Bank Exchange Rate × (1 – tax rate). Assuming sales of $150,000, and a tax rate of 50 percent, the services of the central facility will cost the firm the same as its present cost of maintaining a cash balance if the bank exchange rate is 3 percent of sales. This is computed as $\$150{,}000 \times .03 \times (1 - .50) = \$2{,}250$. The indifference point is thus reached when the exchange costs under the two systems are equal. At this point, the bank exchange rate is designated as the *indifference* bank exchange rate or "*IXR*." This equality is illustrated as

$$ACB \times CC = S \times IXR \times (1 - TR)$$

where: ACB = Average Cash Balance
CC = Cost of Capital

$S =$ Sales
$IXR =$ Indifference Bank Exchange Rate
$TR =$ Tax Rate.

If the IXR is set forth as the dependent variable, its value may be determined as:

$$IXR = \frac{ACB \times CC}{S \times (1 - TR)} .$$

Using the illustrative figures,

$$IXR = \frac{\$15{,}000 \times .15}{\$150{,}000 \times (1 - .50)}$$

$$IXR = .03.$$

A cost comparison of the two exchange systems indicates that under the self-administered system where an average cash balance of $15,000 is maintained, the cost is $2,250. Cost under the centralized system as computed is also $2,250. Thus, if the bank exchange rate is 3 percent of sales, the firm would be indifferent as to which exchange system is employed. As the Actual Bank Exchange Rate decreases relative to the Indifference Bank Exchange Rate, it becomes desirable to adopt the new system.

It is a purpose of this study to further develop this form of analysis to include all the variables affecting the costs associated with the financial exchange function. Time costs of accounts receivable and marketable securities must be introduced. Variable costs of clerical work, credit investigation, credit losses, and interest expense also must be recognized. With the completed expression of these relationships, it will be possible to determine that point at which it becomes advisable for the firm to adopt the services of the centralized system. Herein lies the primary usefulness of the results of this study.

A secondary use of the results of this study should be realized by those currently involved in the planning and implementation of an integrated exchange system. The method of analysis developed in this study is capable also of determining the maximum *charge* which could be assessed by the new system without negatively affecting the firm's financial position. It remains then for the banking community to determine whether the new system is operationally feasible within this cost limit.

II

The Nature of the Exchange Function

The exchange mechanism has progressed through many stages of development while performing its function in an economy of increasing specialization. These stages began with the exchange of real goods and gradually moved through increasing degrees of abstraction. To provide a perspective for the introduction of the checkless society, Livingston stated that:

> Ever since man began to deal with his fellow man, there has been need for a payments mechanism. The nature of this mechanism has evolved from the barter system through the exchange of gold or silver to printed money, and finally to checkbook money. The check has become a relatively recent addition to this evolutionary process.[1]

Accompanying all of these systems have been various benefits and costs. Benefits have continued to arise from the ability to intensify the processes of specialization. Individual and collective costs have been incurred to generate this ability. Throughout this development, rationality has dictated that the point be sought where these benefits and costs are optimized. At this point the exchange function is performed with the highest degree of efficiency. Any alteration in the method of exchange would cause a decline in its utility. Yet possible alterations must be scrutinized continually to insure the existence of the optimal solution.

The concept of an integrated financial exchange system administered by the banking structure again gives rise to the need for such scrutiny. A Federal Reserve survey shows that:

> In addition to the present substantial costs of processing checks by the banking system, commercial enterprises also spend billions of dollars annually for billing, accounts receivable, determining credit ratings, and preparing, mailing and processing checks. These functions can be simplified by employing the checkless society concept of moving funds.[2]

This chapter provides a basis for the ensuing analysis by abstracting the benefits and costs of any exchange system and presenting a range of possible cost solutions. It will be shown that the benefit-cost relationships offered by the developing capacities of automated equipment as employed by the checkless society concept are increasing the feasibility of its implementation for the *collective* exchange needs of the economy. In later chapters, a method will be presented for determining the point at which it becomes desirable for the *individual* firm to actually adopt such a system.

The Utility of Exchange

The utility of the exchange function is derived from the assertion that specialization of activity generates productive efficiency. Specialization of activity and concentration of resources have been shown pragmatically to produce a product whose value is greater than the sum of its individual parts. Economies of specialization are present.

To realize economies resulting from specialization, the exchange function is implied. Time and resources are limited and possessed by the several economic units. To achieve productive economies, these values must be concentrated through a redistribution among the units. The accounting and facilitating of this redistribution of values may be described as the process of exchange. The extent to which increases in value result from combining economic resources is a measure of the utility of exchange. This process facilitates specialization. Productive economies result.

Exchange is not, however, without cost. The process of exchange, itself, requires the use of time and other limited resources. Physical movement and interruption of alternative time uses may be necessary.

Such activities represent specific efforts and sacrifices that are devoted directly to the function of exchange. There are accompanying costs. Thus the problem becomes one of obtaining the benefits of specialization of activity at the expense of exchange costs incurred. From a marginal analysis standpoint, these exchange efforts should be continued to the point where resulting specialization benefits cease to accrue. Here the expected value of the exchange effort is equal to the expected value of the benefits received. The problem, therefore, is to determine the expected value of the benefits to be received from the combination of resources and weigh these benefits against the expected value of the costs incurred to make the combination possible. This is a finite solution. It represents the optimal investment of economic resources in the function of financial exchange.

The Mechanism of Exchange

With the premises that economic resources are limited and specialization of activity results in economies, the questions may now be asked, what form should the exchange mechanism assume in order to maximize its contribution to the production of the economy? How much of the limited resource values should be devoted to the exchange function? What costs are incurred to generate productive economies?

For an exchange to be completed, three abstract processes must occur. First, it is necessary for suppliers and demanders of exchanges to gain access to each other. Economic values produced by the several units must become visible or accessible to the interested parties at the lowest cost. Next, the propriety of the possessions being offered by the exchangers must be identified and value must be verified. Finally, assuming the satisfactory completion of the first two processes, the exchange must be executed transferring the economic value from one unit to another.

Traditionally, money has facilitated the three processes of exchange. An early definition of money comes from St. Thomas Aquinas with reference to Aristotle's work:

> Now money, according to the Philosopher was invented chiefly for the purpose of exchange. . . . Again, the quality of a thing that comes into human use is measured by the price given for it, for which purpose money was invented as stated in the Ethics.
>
> To the end that the products of various workers may be equated and exchange thus made possible, all those goods which can be exchanged must

be made comparable to each other in some way so that the greater or lesser value of each can be known. To this end, money—that is, coin—was invented by which the prices of such things are measured.[3]

A modern writer simplifies but maintains these old ideas by defining money as "anything which is in general use in a given community as a medium of exchange and/or a unit of reckoning."[4]

Thus it can be seen from these definitions of money that its primary functions are to provide an exchange medium and a unit of common measure. Money also acts as a store of value while awaiting further exchanges.

With respect to the three abstract processes of exchange, money provides the necessary requisites. It guarantees liquidity or the capability for exchange. It represents a form of economic value which is generally acceptable thus fulfilling the access function of exchange. The money, itself, identifies its holder as possessing this value and verifies the amount of value involved with the figures printed on its face. Finally, the mere transferring of the money executes the exchange.

Although money in its familiar form is a sufficient condition to perform the processes of exchange, it is not a necessary condition. There are innumerable forms and combinations of related costs associated with the three processes of the exchange mechanism which may be employed. The extent to which any one process is employed is a function of the benefits expected to result from increased productivity, or savings resulting from the reduction of other exchange costs. To illustrate these relationships, three examples of non-money exchange mechanisms will be presented: a barter system, a token commodity system, and a computerized credit system as posed by the checkless society.

Barter

In a barter economy, the exchange mechanism consists of the physical meeting of the holders of value. At this level, benefits from exchange are relatively limited. Specialization is only beginning. Opportunities for alternative time and resource uses are not widely sought out. Hence, to obtain these limited benefits the least cost combination of the three exchange processes is realized by the meeting of the holders and demanders of value. They gain access to each other through meeting and direct communication. They identify each other on a face-to-face basis and verify the values of their respective goods. Tangible evidence of this value is reflected by the real goods themselves. Finally, assuming agreement on the propriety of the offer, physical exchange of these real goods is made.

Such an exchange system is exclusively of a transactions nature. For such an exchange to occur, the benefits accruing to the exchangers must be greater than the efforts devoted to the exchange. Costs are incurred as the exchange takes place. They are current costs which arise in the form of opportunities forgone to generate value alternatively. No fixed facilities are used; no "liquidity risk" is therefore present.

The Token Commodity System

Progressing to a further developed exchange mechanism, it may be recognized by the producing units that even greater productive economies could be realized if it were possible to further specialize productive processes and concentrate resources. Yet to do so requires additional exchanges. These are conflicting uses of resources. To solve this dilemma, economies are sought out in the exchange process itself. Specialization in exchange occurs by creating fixed facilities designed to make the exchange process more efficient. Means are devised to reduce the proportion of resources devoted to gaining access to potential exchangers. They are devised to identify and verify the values being offered. Finally, they are devised to reduce the proportional costs of executing the exchange. Such economies enable the producing units to benefit from specialization in their primary productive activity. With the creation of such fixed or specialized facilities comes the risk that their capacity is too great or too small. This is referred to as liquidity risk.

A method for specializing the exchange processes is the token commodity system. A commodity is arbitrarily designated by the parties to exchanges as a common token of exchange. The commodity itself identifies its holder as possessing value expressed in generalized terms. This value is derived from the agreement and trust that it will be accepted. Such trust is kept because it generates mutual economies by furthering productive efficiency and eliminating previously used exchange procedures which consumed a greater proportion of economic resources.

The discarded procedures and related costs are replaced by costs associated with the token commodity. In addition to the "current" costs of exchanging the token commodity, two further elements of cost are now present in the form of liquidity risk. First, there is a "prepaid" or "time" cost embodied in the commodity. Such a commodity also had to be created from the limited array of resources existing in the economy. It therefore represents value which could have been used alternatively, but now finds utility in facilitating exchange needs. It is the continued forfeiting of the alternative uses of this value which represents a cost to its holder. Hence the risk is taken that this cost will not be recovered or that this liquidity provision is unnecessarily maintained. This is the first element of liquidity risk—over or under capacity.

The other element of liquidity risk concerns the stability of value of the token commodity. By accepting the token commodity, it may become unacceptable in the future and fail to represent the values presumed to be embodied in it. As such, the value believed to be gained from productive efficiencies expires. The holder of the commodity is therefore left with only its value as a real good. The extent to which this risk is taken is a function of the benefits to be derived from further specialization and the existence of integrity and trust in the community. The token exchange mechanism designating a commodity with a relatively high real or alternative value exhibits only a limited degree of trust. Although further risk could be assumed by releasing the real value of the token commodity for alternative use, to do so would cause the expected value of the exchange mechanism to fall below the expected value of the resulting productive economies.

Before leaving the token commodity exchange mechanism and its related costs, a further relationship should be noted. This concerns the mix of costs incurred for the three processes of exchange and risk—all pitted against the benefits which they generate. As resources devoted to gaining access to exchangers, identification and verification of value, and execution are increased, risk is reduced. Yet at the same time, this added effort to reduce risk and thereby increase the expected value of the benefit is performed at the expense of alternative production. A solution to this dilemma again lies in the development of even greater economies in the exchange processes themselves. If means can be created which are more efficient in the processes of exchange, the proportion of resources devoted to exchange is reduced. The further development of these economies is seen in the final exchange mechanism to be presented—a computerized system based on credit.

The Computerized Exchange System

An exchange mechanism based on credit continues to fulfill the three requisites of the exchange process. In this instance, however, the elements of trust and integrity hold more significance. Credit is created. This results when the present value of the future benefits to be gained from an exchange are greater than the present value of the future costs of exchange. If it is possible to gain access, identify and verify future value to be received, and execute the exchange at an expected cost which is lower than the expected benefit, an exchange will occur. Risk is high.

It is this risk that Mitchell of the Federal Reserve Board refers to when commenting on the continuing problem of stability of money and the change from a precious metal system to more advanced systems. "We are still very much occupied with that problem though our reliance for stability is shifting from precious metals to men and institutions."[5]

To minimize this risk, further resources may be devoted to the processes of exchange. Provision may be made for increasing access to exchangers or greater efforts may be devoted to the identification and verification of values being offered. These efforts reduce the risk of accepting false value but, again, they incur costs. Thus, if risk and other exchange costs are to be kept at a level allowing for further specialization to occur, greater efficiencies must be developed in the exchange processes. As these efficiencies are developed, the feasibility of further exchange is increased.

The developing capacities of automated equipment present a means for increasing the efficiency of the exchange processes and reducing risk. No longer is it necessary for a party to an exchange to present and identify himself, or verify the value he is offering with a real or token commodity. These functions can now be performed more efficiently with computers acting as fixed facilities designed to perform the processes of exchange. Each party to exchange has a unique means of identification. Access and communication can be performed electronically. Values and integrity can be verified by readily accessible historical data, and the exchange can be executed and recorded instantly.

The computerized exchange system based on credit implies a new view of money or operating liquidity. The medium of exchange is now largely provided by the hardware and software of the computer system and its ability to perform the three processes of the exchange function. If the ability to add value by a firm or individual is validated by the computer system, liquidity is guaranteed and traditional forms of money are not needed. This "old" money is freed for alternative investment.

The Range of Cost Solutions: Conclusion

Progressing from a barter exchange system to one based on credit and computer capacity, the extremes in cost solutions to this need have been presented. The barter system poses a completely current or variable cost solution. Costs are incurred as needed. Flexibility is present.

At the other extreme, the computerized mechanism is essentially a time cost or prepaid cost solution to the exchange needs of the collective economy. With the specialized exchange information that can be stored and retrieved concerning the credit standings of its users, and the instant access which exchangers have to each other, the risk of executing an unworthy exchange is greatly reduced. With this capability emerges a new type of cost and liquidity risk which is embodied in the investment in the computer network. This investment may be too great or too small, thus causing inefficiency and waste for the total system.

For the individual user, however, the computerized system offers a degree of flexibility which approaches that of the barter system. To recover the costs of the computerized system, the user pays for the exchange service as he uses it through the discounting of sales procedure. He is thus freed from the problems concerning the efficiency of the exchange mechanism and can concentrate on creating value in his primary activity.

At the present time the feasibility of implementing a computerized exchange mechanism is being seriously considered by the banking industry. With the present and future capabilities of automated equipment, this step in the evolution of the exchange mechanism assumes a position of relative imminence. Accompanying it is the opportunity to increase the total product of the firm and the economy.

III

The Development of Specialization in Exchange

Although it can be shown that the concepts associated with a checkless society are capable of fulfilling the theoretical requisites of an economy's exchange system, their operational relevance and feasibility remain in question. In recent months, the prospect of such an exchange system has generated a surge of interest, speculation, and uncertainty. To many, it appears as an irresponsible attempt to innovote solely for the sake of innovation. It is too sudden—too radical.

Yet, in fact, the operational concepts underlying the checkless society have not emerged suddenly. They are not radical. Rather, they have been progressing gradually since approximately 1950 when computers were introduced to the banking industry. Since that time, the developing capacities of automated equipment continually have been scrutinized and adapted to solving the financial exchange needs of the economy. Economies of specialization have resulted in profitable operations for those who have participated in this movement.

At the present time, the further specialization of the banking function is being considered by the leaders in the industry. Efforts are being made to determine the feasibility of extending the application of computer technology to solving the exchange needs of the economy.

These efforts are the latest in a series of orderly events designed to maintain an efficient exchange system. The purposes of this chapter are to trace the development of events leading to the formation of the concept of an operating checkless society, and to place current developments in their proper perspective. It will be shown that the development of these ideas has resulted largely from the processes of increasing specialization and related technological capacity. The chronology of this development assumes three major phases: fragmentary contributions, the bank card concept, and the integrated financial exchange system or checkless society.

Phase One: Fragmentary Contributions

Traditionally, the firm has viewed its bank as a source of services associated with efforts to manage its liquidity effectively. The bank's contribution was generally limited to that of paying checks and providing occasional short-term loans. In return, it was compensated with revenues derived from its control of the firm's bank balance.

Beginning in the 1950's with the introduction of the "first generation" computers, banks began to offer the business community a wider variety of services designed to increase the efficiencies of liquidity management. These services were unrelated to each other. They were fragmentary contributions.

Primary among these contributions were the lock box system and wire transfers for the collection of receivables, the draft as a method of payment, and the committed line of credit as a source of short-term credit. Paralleling the development of these services was the change in method of compensation from the firm's bank balance to the variable service fee. It was these piecemeal developments which began the movement toward the ultimate formation of the concept of the central exchange function. In this section, these initial developments will be presented.

Collections: The Lock Box System and Wire Transfer

In the firm's interest of reducing its level of resources allocated to the exchange function, innovative bankers departed from customary banking services and offered the "lock box system." An early reference to this method of speeding the collection of cash appeared in 1957 under the name of the "Regional Check Clearing Plan." The article states that:

Recent competitive developments in commercial banking have led a leading bank in New York to conduct a publicity campaign for its Regional Check Clearing Plan. . . . One basic aim of any check clearing system is to provide usable funds for depositors in a fast and error free manner. The Regional Check Clearing Plan is designed to give the depositor the use of funds from customers' remittances earlier than might otherwise be possible.[1]

This article describes the plan as having a lock box in a post office near a bank. Incoming funds are mailed to the post office rather than to the company. The box is emptied at regular intervals during the business day by a bank employee. Checks are processed the same day and credited to the company's account, thus providing the prompt availability of the funds.

Another advantage of the lock box service was described as follows:

Using a bank for the check receiving function of a cashier's office cannot eliminate the required cash and accounts receivable procedures, but it can remove some of the work load of existing personnel. Savings in clerical time and the releasing of office help for other work are valuable. . . . In addition, previously compiled remittance lists will save time when accounts receivable are posted and all but miscellaneous receipts can be taken from the cashier's work schedule.[2]

In conjunction with the lock box system, the transfer of funds across long distances also was receiving attention by bankers and cash managers. Rather than use the time consuming and costly mailing services for such transfers, wire transfer systems of the Federal Reserve Banks and private wire systems connecting the major banks of the country were being adapted to the movement of corporate funds. In the late fifties, for example, the New York Life Insurance Company and its 206 branches had a network of 218 bank accounts scattered throughout the United States and Canada.[3] This network, together with the lock box system greatly facilitated their collection of receivables.

Thus the offering of the Regional Check Clearing Plan in the mid-fifties, now commonly known as the lock box system, represents an early movement toward expanded banking services. Recognizing the benefits and costs to the two parties concerned, it remained to be seen whether mutual economies could, in fact, be achieved.

Recent developments. A recent study of the lock box system was conducted by Pinches and reported in the *Credit and Financial Management* periodical. The study included a sample of banks selected from *Fortune's* list of the largest fifty banks in the United States. It reports considerable growth in the lock box service. "Increases were noted in both number of customers using the service, and in dollar amounts handled since the service was first offered. . . . Numbers of customers using lock boxes ranged from 40 to 405 and total monthly remittances processed ranged from $61 million to $500 million."[4]

Since the original offering of the system, the intervening decade has brought with it many modifications—modifications indicative of improved technological capabilities.[5] Most of the variations were designed to further reduce the company's work activity associated with processing receipts of funds. Such services as photocopies of documents, sorting plans, and wire transfers are typically provided by the banks. Two of the more recent plans appear to be linked closely with the computer capabilities of banks. They offer remittance information through punched cards, or paper or magnetic tape compatible with the company's computer system. This provides for automatic updating of records.

A second variation includes data transmission. Accordingly, information concerning remittances can be wired daily or more frequently directly to the company's computing center over telephone lines. This is the most advanced system now in use. Data are transmitted in a variety of machinable forms, including core to core, card to card, magnetic tape, and other.

Payments: The Draft

The use of the draft is another illustration of the efforts of the banking and business communities to reduce the total costs associated with financial exchanges. This method of payment replaces the check. The draft is not paid by the bank until it is accepted by the drawer. As a result, no funds have to be left on deposit to cover it until arrival at the issuer's bank.

In a survey conducted by the *Wall Street Journal* in 1961, the participants viewed the use of drafts as follows:

> The advantage of using drafts, these companies say, is that they reduce the number and size of regional bank accounts and the amount of money they have "floating" in the form of checks. This reduces their working capital needs and permits corporate treasurers to squeeze more income from money that ordinarily would be reposing in bank accounts awaiting the arrival of checks drawn against them.[6]

The use of drafts gained limited use in the late 1950's and early 1960's. Canada Dry Corporation was reported to be one of the first companies to adopt this payment system. When it instituted the system, Canada Dry eliminated all of its checking accounts outside New York, and paid by draft on a New York bank.[7] Other large firms such as American Telephone and Telegraph also use the draft system to economize in the management of cash.[8]

Although the use of drafts decreases the cash balance maintained by the firm and thereby reduces time costs, this efficiency for the firm is gained almost entirely at the expense of banks. Reduced bank balances eliminate major sources of income for the bank. As a result, the initial reaction to drafts by bankers was unfavorable. According to Federal Reserve officials, a basic problem was that "a widening use of drafts would represent a setback to the banking system's attempt to speed up check handling with electronic equipment.[9]

This view, presented in 1961, was apparently an accurate one. Banks immediately moved to establish a rate structure for the draft service, which thwarted its further growth. The First National Bank of Birmingham, Alabama, for instance, normally would not cash a company's draft unless the firm had a compensating balance there. The South Side Atlanta Bank would not cash drafts of companies located beyond the immediate business area. Some banks imposed cashing fees as high as 50 cents per draft.[10]

Since the draft service was not compatible with the bank's developing automated operations, its use remained limited. Insurance companies and common carriers were the exceptions. In these industries, other advantages made the costs charged by the banks tolerable.

Recently the banking system has responded to the needs of certain industries by introducing automated systems to handle the processing of drafts at lower costs. At the beginning of 1966, the Chicago Clearing House Association began electronic operations for clearing drafts representing freight bills.[11] The plan is known as the Chicago Consolidated Freight Payment Plan. The agreeing banks supply each other with names and identification numbers of the banks and the account numbers of all carriers and shippers having arrangements with them.

Burroughs Clearing House reports that "this innovation–paying freight bills through an established clearing house–is a breakthrough in automated bill paying that may eventually be adopted by other clearing houses."[12] This introduction of automated draft services for bill settlement may lead to the wider use of the service. It represents another movement toward the creation of a service package offered by banks in the attempt to gain efficiencies in the financial exchange function.

Source of Liquidity: Formal Line of Credit

The firm's relationship with its bank has traditionally been viewed as that of a quasi-insurer of short-run liquidity. Given reasonable credit standings, and uses of the bank's other services, the firm can generally rely on its bank to partially absorb the liquidity needs associated with precautionary motives for holding cash balances. This informal relationship has long been recognized by writers of cash management theory. One author stated this relationship as follows:

> The determination of the size of the bank balances that a firm maintains cannot be considered a science—it is an imperfect art. It is an art, however, in which the money manager must appraise the value of its banking relationship and weigh it against the possible income that can be earned on balances in excess of some irreducible minimum.[13]

By reasoning in this manner, the firm is able to reduce its cash balance while the bank stands ready to extend short-term loans when unexpected cash needs arise. To provide this service, the banks must continuously be in a less than "loaned-up" position. The bank costs associated with this position have traditionally been covered by income from compensating balances.

In a questionnaire completed by 200 companies with assets in excess of $100 million, responses concerning bank relationships and services appear to support this relationship. This study reports that the service mentioned most frequently by corporate officers is "the insurance service that their banks provide."[14]

More recently, firms and banks have recognized this service in a more formal manner. With the newly acquired computer capacity providing for the more accurate measurement of the costs and benefits to both parties, agreements for formal lines of credit and related commitment fees have become more widely used.[15] This enables the firm to reduce its cash balance while being assured that unexpected cash needs will be covered. The bank is directly compensated for this service via a commitment fee. Such fees are customarily computed on the daily portion of the unused maximum amount of the total credit available during the term of the agreement.[16]

The Federal Reserve Bank of Philadelphia reports that in recent years "more companies have begun to rely on lines of credit with banks to supply funds fast, rather than keeping cash on deposit. . . . They're doing so . . . just as a lot of individuals with pre-established lines of credit at banks . . . are almost relying on them as a source of spending money."[17]

An economist of the Irving Trust Company comments that:

> . . . some companies have found it hazardous to count on credit lines. Frequently, firms have found what was thought to be an open credit line in a bank is actually closed, because the bank lacks the funds to satisfy its commitments. To make sure they're not left out in the cold this way, there recently has been a surprisingly large shift among such firms from an informal understanding to formal credit in exchange for a commitment fee.[18]

Change in fee structures. During the development of these services, conventional practices for receiving compensation by banks also began to be restructured. Traditionally, banks have relied on controlling the firm's balance as a source of compensation. Banking was originally aimed at the financially powerful individual or business organization and offered few services relative to the level of bank balances maintained.[19] As a result of the modest number of services requested and the generous profits gained from these balances, banks traditionally have offered ancillary services without explicit charges.

However, as banks began to offer a greater variety and quantity of services, especially those produced by electronic data-processing equipment,[20] bank costs increased and bank balances decreased. This squeeze is stated in one article as follows:

> With the new techniques of lock box collection systems, wire transfer of funds, the draft, and other methods of faster money mobilization that have been developed in recent years . . . the corporation can operate with less cash tied up in demand balances. This reduction is at the expense of the banks all over the country that used to have several days float time.[21]

These combined pressures of reduced balances and added costs have forced the banks to reconsider their method for receiving compensation. To cover the banks' costs in the traditional manner, compensating balances would have to be extremely high. The result of these developments is that "there is a growing belief among executives of the nation's larger banks that within the next few years an ancient and cherished custom of American banking, 'compensating balance,' will be on its way out and will be succeeded by some kind of a metered or fee system."[22]

Fee systems are already commonly associated with the lock box system. Although compensating balances are still widely used, many banks apply a service charge. One survey reports that "there is no one standard formula for charging or paying for the service. Roughly, the cost per check received in the lock box is most often in the range of 10 to 25 cents per item."[23]

As has already been noted, there is also a growing practice in fee arrangements for the draft service and the committed line of credit.

Phase one—concluded. Several developments have been identified as departures from traditional banking practices. The lock box system, the electronic transfer of funds, the draft, and the line of credit, all associated with increased automated capabilities, represent fragmentary solutions for gaining economies in activities related to the function of financial exchange. Together with these developments, the traditional practice of the compensating balance has given way to a variable fee structure directly associated with the services offered. Thus, with these fragmentary developments breaking traditional lines, the setting has been established for a major movement toward an integrated financial exchange system.

Phase Two: The Bank Credit Card

With the increased automated capacities of banks and the experience of offering innovative services for interfirm transactions, bankers were prepared to extend their services to firm-consumer transactions. This was done with the widespread offering of bank credit cards which gained notable momentum in 1965. With the credit card movement came the banks' major thrust into the broader concept of financial exchange.

The plans offered to retailers and consumers contained, again, the elements of rapid collection for the seller, the draft as a medium for payment, the formal line of credit, and inter-bank communications. However, instead of being offered as individual services, they were now recognized as a package of related services accompanied by a structure of variable service fees. It is the purpose of this section to describe the bank card system as it relates to the function of financial exchange and to indicate the direction of its development.

Origin of the Concept

Although the concept of a bank credit card has come into widespread usage only recently, its introduction occurred over twenty years ago. In 1946, a Brooklyn bank developed a community credit plan known as "Charg-It."[24] In 1950, this plan was introduced by the Paterson Savings and Trust Company, Paterson, New Jersey. Many writers agree that the Charg-It plan was the first of its kind offering some entirely new concepts in commercial banking.[25]

The plan was basically a form of revolving credit offered by the bank. After passing a thorough investigation by the bank, the applicant would be issued scrip drafts for the amount of his agreed line of credit. The individual was then able to make purchases at the participating retail stores using the scrip as payment. At the end of each day, the merchant turned the scrip over to the bank and received immediate credit for the sales. From that point on, it was the bank's responsibility to collect from the individual. Bills were mailed monthly covering all purchases made at the participating stores. As compensation, the bank discounted the scrip by 8 percent. In addition, an interest charge of one-half of 1 percent per month was placed on the credit users' unpaid balances.[26]

In 1951, the Franklin National Bank of Rockville Center, New York, offered a modified Charg-It plan, which has since remained the model for most current bank plans.[27] The modification was the replacement of scrip with a sales slip. At the end of the business day, the merchants took the sales slips to the bank and got immediate deposit credit for their total value minus the agreed discount. The sales slips thus served as a legal draft to support the accounts receivable held by the bank.

Currently, a leading bank card operation is the Bank Americard plan offered in California by the Bank of America.[28] The services provided by this operation are similar to those introduced in the early 1950's. The consumer receives his Bank Americard without charge after careful credit screening. He has automatic charge privileges with over 38,000 businesses. Statements are mailed monthly for all charges made, and the only cost to him is incurred if settlement is not made within 25 days. At that time, a charge of 1½ percent per month is added. The merchant's cost is the draft discount which generally ranges from 1 percent to 5 percent.

The Services of Charge Account Banking

Although the prime motivation of the bankers for introducing these plans is the profit to be gained from financing consumer credit, retail businesses and consumers also realize several advantages. These advantages are very similar to those derived from the services offered for interfirm transactions. A major benefit to the participating merchant is the collection mechanism. Since the credit function is assumed by the bank, all sales are for cash. Thus the cash cycle is speeded up allowing for greater efficiency in performing the firm's primary function—merchandising.

Secondly, since the bank is in control of the credit process, it assumes many costs previously incurred by the merchant. These include the costs of credit investigation, bookkeeping costs for receivables, collection expenses, and the losses resulting from uncollectible accounts. Accompanying the elimination of these variable expenses is the freeing of administrative time and related fixed costs for direction to other uses.

Finally, the availability of credit for consumers permits many small businesses previously financially unable to finance a credit operation to cater to a wider market of customers.

From the consumer's standpoint, a major convenience of the credit card plan is the availability of the credit itself. With the formal line of credit, the consumer has a reliable source of liquidity thereby reducing the need for maintaining precautionary cash balances.

Further, the use of the draft eliminates the need for a bank balance. So long as the drafts are paid within a relatively short period such as 25 days, no service charges are added.

The Bank Americard plan describes the following advantages:

> Membership is an obvious convenience to the consumer and business alike. For the consumer, it's an automatic charge account with monthly billing only, with deferred payment privileges. So it's simplified budgeting and bookkeeping. For the business it's instant cash, since the sales slips can be immediately credited to its account at the nearest Bank of America office. Moreover, it's instant credit control, for the bank assumes the checking and collection obligations. So it frees the business of worry and of having capital tied up in customer receivables.[29]

Thus, the concept of charge account banking offers a package of services to the merchant and consumer. In return, the bank is compensated with the variable charges based on the volume of transactions handled and the amount of credit outstanding. It is for the merchant to balance the benefits received from these services with his discount rate to determine the advisability of participating in such a plan. Similarly, the consumer has the choice of the utility of current consumption and related interest charges; or delayed, interest-free consumption. In both cases, time values of money are relevant to the decision.

Progress of the Bank Credit Card Concept

The initial progress of the bank credit card concept was slow. After a decade of experience in 1958, there were only approximately 60 banks offering the plan.[30] This number increased in 1959 to nearly 100 as the result of the entry of the Chase Manhattan Bank of New York and the Bank of America in California. With the entry of these two prestigious banks, the doubts of the traditionally conservative banking community were quelled. Charge account banking had finally been approved by the banking community.

The success of the programs, however, remained in serious question. In 1962, the Chase Manhattan Bank sold its credit card business due to unsatisfactory profit performance.[31] As reported by *Forbes,* the plan was unsuccessful due to resistance from the major credit plans operated by New York's large department stores.[32] These stores use their credit plans as a form of market discrimination and refused to release this competitive advantage. As a result, the bank's plan did not achieve a sufficient volume of transactions to cover its high cost.

Although success in the bank credit card field was not automatic, the other large entrant in the field in 1959, the Bank of America, has emerged as a leader. By 1962 its operation became profitable. In December, 1968, the Bank of America plan had some 16.8 million card holders with 397,000 participating merchants.[33]

The administrators of the plan point out that there are two basic requisites which must be met if a plan is to survive: volume and controls. "Volume is basic to the economic use of electronic equipment to take over paper work. Controls are basic to avoidance of costly collection problems."[34]

It seems apparent that some plans were unable to meet these two requisites for success. In addition to the failure of the Chase Manhattan plan, many others failed, reducing the number in mid-1965 to only 75. Since that time, however, there has been a dramatic surge in offerings bringing the number of participants in bank sponsored card programs in January, 1969, to approximately 3,000.[35]

Indeed, there are many factors related to volume and cost controls which have contributed to the increase in the number of plans. These include consumer and merchant attitudes, and the major item of cost. One notable development related to cost is the decline in the merchant's discount rate. Original plans discounted the sales draft by 8 percent.[36] In 1955, as reported by the Cole study, the fee ranged from 5 percent to 8 percent with the average being between 5 percent and 6 percent.[37] In 1959, the Hofmann study also states the average rate as being between 5 percent and 6 percent.[38] Even as late as 1963, the study by Patterson reported the rate to range from 5 percent to 7 percent.[39]

More recently, however, and paralleling the dramatic increase in the number of plans, the rate has decreased. The Bank of America's rate structure originally ranged from 3 percent to 5 percent. "This charge is based on the type of business—five percent for liquor stores, service stations; four percent for restaurants and hotels; three percent for most businesses."[40] The rate has since declined to as low as one percent.

It appears from the chronology of the changes in discount rates that the departure from the lengthy 5 percent to 6 percent plateau to lower rates paralleled two other developments: the widespread use by banks of automated processing equipment and the increase in offerings of credit card operations. Thus again there appears to be some correlation between the economies offered by automated equipment and the offering of innovative services by banks.

Bank Credit Cards in Transition: Central Exchange

The final developments in Phase Two—the bank credit card service—are assuming their posture at the present time. The original notion of a bank credit card offered to serve the local market area of the bank has been put aside. It is now being recognized that there are greater economies to be derived from automated equipment and communications capabilities which can be realized by consolidating local plans into regional plans, and finally a centralized national plan.

At the present time, there are four distinct movements by banks to develop regional and national credit card plans. The first among these movements was initiated by the Bank of America. In May of 1966 it announced plans to establish a nation-wide credit card system.[41] Under this plan, banks throughout the country will enter into licensing agreements. Each bank will administer its Bank Americard plan independently, maintaining control over credit policies, rates, and promotion. The card will be usable in any area where the plan is in effect, regardless of where it is issued. Systems will be developed to handle the clearing of sales drafts between all issuing banks.

The second movement toward regional and national development was also initiated in California. Four banks have formed the California Bankcard Association and set up a central clearing house to handle the exchange of charge transactions and to maintain credit information on cardholders.[42] By the middle of 1968, the banks expect a potential of 1.2 million cardholders and 30,000 participating merchants.

The third movement is known as the Midwest Bank Card system with headquarters in Chicago. In January, 1967, the MBC had commitments with some 450 banks and 30,000 merchants. Estimates are that the MBC banks will issue 6 million credit cards. Sales drafts will be exchanged among the banks similar to the present methods for handling checks.

The final and most exciting movement is known as Interbankard, Inc. This group includes major banks in Pittsburgh, Richmond, Atlanta, Buffalo, and Phoenix. Representatives from both the Midwest Bank Card and California Bankcard groups have been in dialogue with the Interbankard system. Indications are that Interbankard will become a national plan:

> Some credit card experts have expressed the opinion that the Interbankard system will provide the framework that ultimately may tie bank credit card programs into a giant network stretching the length and breadth of the nation, and later on, to countries abroad.
>
> Initially the program calls for the interchange of cards and merchants tickets. . . . In the future, . . . data centers will be established that will record and transmit such information electronically.[43]

Thus, indications are that the bank credit card system may lead to a massive centralized system for handling financial exchanges. At the present time, if all existing bank credit card programs merged into one system, the result would be a network of regional banks with an aggregation of 20 to 30 million cardholders. In a recent speech by the president of Interbankard, there were implications "that the so-called checkless society is not as distant as many financial people even as little as six months ago once thought, and the wherewithal—the apparatus for entry into it—is indeed at hand."[44]

Phase Three: Integrated Financial Exchange System

The first and second phases in the development of ideas relating to financial exchanges may be described as periods of arousal. The banking community was stirred by the demonstrated demand of firms and consumers for increased economy in the timing and execution of money settlements. Effective response to these demands has been feasible through the use of automated equipment. Innovative ideas and advanced technological capacity are now embodied in the numerous banking services offered to businesses. The bank credit card is being used extensively by the consumer.

Yet the complete integration of these services offered by banking institutions is not yet an operational reality. Even though the financial exchange needs of both business and the consumer are composed of common elements, the two groups have been viewed by bankers as being quite separate. This separateness is demonstrated by the array of banking services being offered at this time. The needs of business are being handled on a fragmentary basis, whereas the consumer is using packaged services. Both approaches are designed to accomplish the same objective: efficient financial exchange.

The final phase in the development of these ideas leads to the integration of financial exchange services for all users. Due to the apparent success of the package approach of the bank credit card offered to the consumer, and the similarity of the needs of business, it is now being recognized that an extension of the package approach should be economically feasible for the handling of all financial exchanges. Again, technological economies offered by automated equipment appear to give rise to this feasibility.

At the present time the nature of the solution to this problem of integration is receiving the unparalleled attention of the banking community. It is a time of extensive speculation, research, and question. The resulting solution will have wide implications for all parties to financial exchanges. Grounded in notions of time values and least-cost solutions, the integrated approach will offer its users the opportunity for a more rational evaluation of the consequences of economic decisions. It is the purpose of this final section to present the most recent developments in the movement toward an integrated solution to financial exchange needs. These developments are represented by descriptions of hypothesized integrated systems, instances of actual implementation, and the nature of research currently in progress.

Hypothesized Integrated Systems

The objective of the financial exchange function is clear: provision for the efficient timing and execution of transfers of wealth. The validity of this objective is demonstrated by the rapid transition of the parties to exchanges from old methods to new methods. Efficiencies are being sought. At the present time, even greater efficiencies are thought to be present by several groups or individuals who have speculated about integrated systems for financial exchange. Among these, the principal groups are the Federal Reserve System, represented by George Mitchell of the Board of Governors and John Clarke of the Federal Reserve Bank of New York; the American Bankers' Association, represented by Dale L. Reistad, its Director of Automation, and W. Putman Livingston of the Bankers Trust Company in New York; and the Bank Administration Institute (BAI, formerly NABAC), represented by Byers Miller. Indications of their conviction as to an integrated exchange system have been abundantly pronounced.

Mitchell has stated that:

> The intricate process of settlement and deposit accounting will be carried on concurrently at and between 250 or so computer centers located throughout the country. . . . Most of this information will be received at the bank in machine language. . . . In this system there is no check sorting and resorting, no shipment of checks . . . no float and a minimum of manual processing. . . . Furthermore, it seems logical and practical that at least some of the customer accounting antecedent and subsequent to settlement could be most economically done in a coordinated package with settlement accounting. . . . Every sales transaction, for example, by specifying a settlement date, might immediately be put into the bank's computer where it could accomplish immediate settlement or subsequent reminder and settlement. Similarly, a bank could handle payrolls and agree to bill many types of contractual payments for insurance, rent, and mortgage payments. In short, by virtue of its central position in the payments process the bank is also able to perform ancillary and antecedent accounting and billing more economically than anyone else.[45]

The Federal Reserve's Subcommittee for Improving the Payments Mechanism, of which John Clarke is chairman, has also hypothesized an integrated exchange system. The chairman recently stated before the Association for Bank Audit, Control, and Operation that:

> My message is uncomplicated: It is that a Direct-Funds-Transfer system seems to be technically, operationally and economically feasible and that it is apparently inevitable. But I am compelled to add that a good deal of hard work and further research including technological, economic, legal, and sociological, must go into various aspects of such a system if it is to become a reality.[46]

One major research project prepared for this subcommittee has already been completed. The study, performed by the Stanford Research Institute, is entitled "A Techno-Economic Study of Methods for Improving the Payments Mechanism."[47] The Direct Funds Transfer System is the term the Institute has given to its integrated system. With reference to this research, Clarke described in detail the possible composition of a DFT system. It postulates the flow of funds through the banking system on a "giro" basis. The payor would directly instruct his bank of deposit to debit his account, thus effecting a transfer to the payor's account. Such transfers would be made by electronic impulses originating in terminals of retail establishments, business offices, and even private residences. There would be approximately 10 to 12 regional centers, 200 to 1,000 local centers, 1 to 4 million terminals, and 100 million account holders to serve a population of 200 million, sales of $400 billion, and 40 to 200 billion transactions. Clarke stated that these figures "are not selected at random but represent some attempt at extending into the future, and applying statistical information available today.[48]

Quoting the report itself, a conclusion is that "by any standard of measurement, the funds transfer system offers significant savings over the present system. Addition of the intangible savings makes the direct funds transfer system even more attractive."[49]

Another study of more limited scope was performed by the Bank Administration Institute and is entitled "An Electronic Network for Check Collection: A Feasibility Study." This research focused its attention on two questions: "Utilizing technology now available, is it possible to develop a practical check collection system that incorporates an electronic network for transmitting check information between banks?" "What would such a system cost?" Published results of the study using check inter-change between 28 commercial banks and two Federal Reserve banks suggests that "construction of a system whereby check information would be forwarded electronically was both feasible and potentially would cost less than current methods."[50]

Such economies are also foreseen by a third leading spokesman in this area, W. Putman Livingston, who is chairman of the American Bankers' Association's Committee on the Checkless Society. He recently stated that "the checkless society undoubtedly holds one of the most significant promises of the computer age: A financial utility dedicated to the movement of money, credit, credit information, and to supplying data for the grist mills of our economists."[51]

Also making reference to the Stanford report, Livingston remarked that:

> The checkless society offers another alternative manner of moving money that may prove to be extremely attractive to banks, business and consumers. . . . Savings to business would come mainly from the facilities of banks to handle the transactions involved in payables and accounts receivable. With funds moving by wire as "instant money," this arrangement has great potential. It will increase the functions of banks, and thus, their income. The checkless society operation will be essentially computer talking to computer.[52]

In addition to the contributions of the Federal Reserve, the American Bankers Association, and the BAI, integrated systems have been postulated by several other individuals. Among the notable contributions are "SAVE,"[53] System for Automatic Value Exchange; "SPACE,"[54] Settlements, Payments, Accounting, Credit Extension; the "M-CARD,"[55] or Money Card system; and the "ELECTRONIC CURRENCY SYSTEM."[56] These systems all have the common elements of the electronic transfer of funds, identification devices, credit information, automatic credit availability, and accounting information. Some provide for the automatic investment of debit balances.

Research in Progress

The Federal Reserve System has several committees working on various aspects of the integrated exchange problem.[57] The Committee on Inter-Bank Electronic Communications is studying intermediate- and longer-range data transmission and electronic processing needs. A sub-area of concentration is the intensive study of the application of data transmission technology to information transfers within the Federal Reserve System and commercial banks. The assignments include the technology of wire transfer of funds and money settlement via computer-to-computer hook-up. These committees are in addition to that chaired by Clarke on the payments mechanism.

The BAI is also conducting major research in this area. In December, 1966, it launched a second and more advanced study.[58] Its objective is to study the possibility of constructing a national electronic network for the entire banking system. This would be used for the electronic exchange of all forms of information. The study will concentrate on cash item data, security data, funds transfers, alert systems, loan and credit information, exchange, and the transmission of general operating data. The director of the association, Byers Miller, has stated that "what is needed is a plan for accomplishing the key technical, economic, and social tasks that 'make or break' the use of a highly integrated technical system."[59]

Finally, the American Bankers' Association's Committee on the Checkless Society has a number of projects currently in progress. Its Personal Identification Project (PIP) is attempting to develop a standard for individual identification.[60] Visual identification, voice identification, and secret coded identification processes are being studied.

The committee is also directing four pilot operations attempting to apply the available technology in its present state of development.[61] The studies are being designed to test the theories thus far presented. They will be performed in communities of less than 250,000 people, have the Touch-Tone telephone system in operation, and have the participation of approximately 50 retailers and 300-400 bank customers. The systems will handle accounts receivable, and provide a preauthorized automatic debit and credit bill paying service.

At present, operating examples of the limited application of a central exchange system are being tested privately by several banks in the East. The first of these is being offered by banks in Pennsylvania and Ohio that are operating a "Checkless Utility Payment Service."[62] In Philadelphia, for example, 25 institutions including all the major banks are participating in an automatic bill paying service developed by the Philadelphia Electric Company and the First Pennsylvania Banking & Trust Company. Some 12,000 customers have authorized their banks to deduct monthly electric bill charges from their accounts and credit these amounts to the Philadelphia Electric Company account. The company views the automatic crediting procedure as speeding up collections and providing more accurate projection of cash flows. The company has received requests for information about the plan from some 30 gas and electric utilities after only several months of operation.

Another illustration of the direct transfer of funds has been introduced by the Hempstead Bank of New York State. Approximately 100 retailers are participating in the bank's "Black Box" demonstration.[63] In each store a small "box" or electronic device is linked to a number of other units with telephone equipment. At the other end is the bank's computer. A plastic card is inserted in the Touch-Tone phone and, via the black box, immediately identifies the customer. The amount of the sale is entered and instantly transfers funds from the customer's account to the merchant's account. The bank discounts the transactions by 1 to 2 percent of the sale and provides automatic credit for its cardholders.

The Integrated System in Perspective

Beyond the cost reductions resulting from the increased efficiency of the exchange mechanism itself, an integrated system also offers the capacity for identifying the costs associated with the timing of an exchange. With instant short-term credit available and the related charges specified, a more accurate cost-benefit analysis is possible for determining the optimal source-use structure of funds. With reference to this advantage, Livingston has stated that:

> The ability of the card to transfer funds from one customer's bank to the store's bank account instantly brings up the question of the time value of money. Does the customer want to pay now or later? The checkless society system will allow him to pay on any day he chooses and will compute the discount or carrying charge accordingly. The payments mechanism in a checkless society will be capable of calculating daily the time value of money for each transaction. It can operate this way on a local and nationwide level.[64]

Similar reference to these advantages is made in a recent article, "Credit Aspects of Total Automation," where the author states that:

> Businesses which extend terms, even one day terms, are in the business of lending money. They must operate credit and collection departments. From an economic standpoint their prices must reflect this. Card-carrying consumers should be able to command a price that excludes the vendor's lending costs. Then it becomes up to the consumer: either he pays from his

own ready reserves or from borrowing, the cost of which is known to him rather than being buried in the purchase price.[65]

The article also views the purchases of vendors as being similar to those of consumers, tracing the line of transactions back to raw materials purchases. In all cases, sales prices include after tax costs for interest, discounts lost, credit and collection efforts and bad debts. Under the integrated exchange system, these costs can be isolated and compared with other available alternatives.

As measurements of cash flows determined by the timing of transactions become more precise, the recognition of time values of wealth will be facilitated. This recognition leads naturally to the assumed goal of the corporation—profit maximization reflecting value added. Mitchell points out that "the bank's service could include a large part of the accounting, analysis, and financing of receivables and even extend to provisions for much current cash flow accounting, a basis of analysis that has become of increasing importance in both business and financial planning."[66]

Conclusion

In this chapter the development of ideas relating to the concept of a centralized financial exchange function has been presented. Beginning with fragmentary contributions designed to facilitate the exchange process, coupled with a departure from traditional means of compensation, banks began to assume their natural role as specialists in financial exchange. Prompted by success in these initial stages, this specialization evolved into a phase of package services embodied in the bank credit card. Finally, the concept of a financial utility designed for the efficient movement of money, credit, and information has overtaken the leaders of the industry. Through research and testing currently in progress, the operational reality of such a concept is expected by the mid-1970's. Created by imaginative theorists and made operationally feasible by the technological capacity of automated equipment, the facility for money settlement of the future is expected to offer unparalleled economies to its users.

To achieve these economies, the format has been made clear. It is the need for detail that remains. As recently stated by the director of the BAI, "I believe that we should do more than question whether or not the checkless society will ever occur, or discuss how soon it might appear. I believe much more progress can be made if we assemble factual data on loads, costs, and potential benefits."[67] It is such detail which this study hopes to contribute.

IV

Development of the Indifference Model

In an economy comprised of many specialized productive units, the function of financial exchange must be performed. As discussed in Chapter II, this function may be performed by each of the units on a barter basis as a part of its productive activity. In this case, each unit assumes the risks for the financial exchange function; each searches for efficiency. Variable costs are incurred as exchanges are made. At the other extreme, only one unit performs the financial exchange function. It specializes in this activity and sells its service to the other units as a factor of production. For a centralized financial exchange system, fixed costs resulting from the continued readiness to serve are incurred. If there are economies of specialization in the performance of the financial exchange function, then the total cost of the specializing unit under the central system will be lower than the sum of the individual costs of the several units using self-administered systems. As economies are developed, it becomes desirable at some point for the several units to cease performing the exchange function themselves, and to begin purchasing this service as a specialized factor in the production of their primary activities.

As a practical matter, the least cost solution to the exchange process will lie between the two all-or-nothing extremes. As opportunities for specialization in the various productive activities increase, the transition progresses from the current cost approach of the barter system to the fixed, centralized approach of the specialized system. For each service-using firm, costs incurred are a mixture of self-administered time costs and current costs for services purchased from exchange specialists.

Chapter III documented the predictions that in the near future the banking community will present to business firms an opportunity to further this transition in the exchange mechanism. The integrated exchange system represents the progression of specialization in the exchange function. It is the purpose of this chapter to present a useful and practical method for evaluating the firm's advisability of changing from current methods of handling the exchange function to newer methods to be offered by the banking system and its automated capabilities. To evaluate the potential economies of a central exchange system, an indifference point model will be developed. The design of this model is presented in this chapter.

Nature of the Indifference Model

General discussions of two alternative cost solutions to the function of financial exchange have been presented: self-administered systems and a proposed central exchange system. Each approach generates the benefits of accomplishing the firm's exchange needs. Each incurs costs. Given the costs associated with the two systems, a point may be determined where the firm is indifferent as to which system of exchange is adopted. This is referred to as the indifference point or the indifference total cost level.

To analyze the costs contributing to the financial exchange function and to formulate a useful indifference decision model, an abstract approach will be followed. This poses extreme situations under restrictive assumptions as outer limits to the range of possible solutions for the exchange function. After the model has been developed under these conditions, consideration will be given to relaxing the several assumptions to accommodate practical business conditions.

The extreme situations to be used for expository purposes range from a traditional system of exchange containing many self-administered variables to one which purchases the *entire* exchange service externally from the central exchange facility. The effect of these extreme systems is reflected in the following two sets of financial statements shown in Figures 2 and 3. In these examples, the "Self-

Figure 2

FINANCIAL STATEMENTS REFLECTING TRADITIONAL EXCHANGE SYSTEM

Balance Sheet
Self-Sufficient Company

CASH	$ xxxx	ACCOUNTS PAYABLE	$ xxxx
MARKETABLE SECURITIES	xxxx	Other Sources	xxxx
ACCOUNTS RECEIVABLE	xxxx		
Real Assets			
	$ xxxx		$ xxxx

Income Statement
Self-Sufficient Company

Sales		$ xxxx
Cost of Goods Sold		xxxx
Gross Profit		xxxx
Expenses:		
Wages	$ xxxx	
Selling	xxxx	
Administrative	xxxx	
BANK EXPENSE	xxxx	
CREDIT DEPT	xxxx	
BAD DEBTS	xxxx	
CASHIERS EXPENSE	xxxx	
DISCOUNTS LOST	xxxx	
Other Expense	xxxx	
Total Expenses		xxxx
Net Operating Income		xxxx
INTEREST INCOME		xxxx
INTEREST EXPENSE		xxxx
Net Income Before Taxes		$ xxxx
Income Taxes		xxxx
Net Income After Taxes		$ xxxx

Figure 3

FINANCIAL STATEMENTS REFLECTING CENTRALIZED SYSTEM

Balance Sheet
Specialized Company

Real Assets	$ xxxxx	BANK CREDIT	$ xxxxx
		Other Sources	xxxxx
	$ xxxxx		
			$ xxxxx

Income Statement
Specialized Company

Sales		$ xxxxx
Cost of Goods Sold		xxxxx
Gross Profit		$ xxxxx
Expenses:		
Wages	$ xxxxx	
Selling	xxxxx	
Administrative	xxxxx	
Other Expenses	xxxxx	
BANK EXCHANGE SERVICE EXPENSE	xxxxx	
BANK CREDIT EXPENSE	xxxxx	
Total Expenses		xxxxx
Net Operating Income		xxxxx
Income Taxes		xxxxx
Net Income After Taxes		$ xxxxx

Sufficient Company" performs most of the exchange function activities itself. The "Specialized Company" buys all exchange function services from the centralized system.

The differences in these statements are the result of changing from traditional methods for handling financial exchanges to the proposed centralized method. To perform the exchange function in the traditional manner, the following accounts are maintained by the "Self-Sufficient" firm: cash, marketable securities, accounts receivable, accounts payable, bank expense, credit department expense, bad debts, cashier's expense, interest income, and interest expense. The "Specializing" firm eliminates the above accounts from its control and replaces them with: bank exchange service expense, bank credit expense or income, and bank credit payable.

Given values for the various accounts of the self-administered firm, the question to be answered by the development of the indifference model is: What amount can the same firm afford to pay for the exchange service without adversely affecting its financial position as measured by return on capital sources? To obtain an answer to this question the above accounts and several other related variables will be included in the formulation of a complete model. The effect of each of the variables will be shown in factoral form by developing the model on a step by step basis until it is completed.

The Variables

The first variable of the self-sufficient firm to be transformed by the indifference model is its average cash balance. This transformation may be achieved by relating four independent variables and one dependent variable. The independent variables are the firm's average cash balance, the average cost of capital, the income tax rate, and sales. The dependent variable is the indifference bank exchange rate.

The Average Cash Balance and the Cost of Capital

The firm has traditionally maintained a positive average cash balance in order to satisfy its transactions needs and precautionary needs for operating liquidity. If, for example, the firm's inflows and outflows of cash repeated the following pattern, its average cash balance would be a positive balance of 10 as shown below:

Time	*Inflow*	*Outflow*	*Self-Administered Balance*
1	20	10	10
2		4	6
3	15	5	16
4		3	13
5		4	9
6	17	8	18
7		10	8
8		8	0
			$80 \div 8 = 10$

The allocation of the firm's sources of funds to maintaining this average asset balance of 10 is accompanied by a cost. This cost is measured by applying the firm's average cost of capital rate indicating the growth rate or earning rate required on each dollar of invested capital.

In the analysis, the following assumptions are made concerning the average cash balance and cost of capital variables.

1) The firm's average cash balance is maintained for transactions-precautionary purposes related to operating receipts and disbursements. The firm does not hoard cash, speculate in it, or finance major capital acquisitions from internally generated cash.
2) The firm's assets homogeneously generate its rate of return. Any single asset may be attributed with the average earning rate.
3) The changeover from the traditional exchange system to the central system does not affect the total risk faced by the firm. Its cost of capital remains constant.
4) The firm's sources of funds, including current liabilities, are homogeneously distributed among the assets. The cost of any single dollar invested in an asset is the average cost of the total sources of funds.

The average cost of capital computation is presented as follows using assumed data.

Source	*Amount*	*Percent of Total*	*Cost After Tax*	*Index*
Current Liab.	$15,000	12.5%	8%	100
Equity	105,000	87.5	16	1,400
		100.0%		1,500

1,500 ÷ 100% = 15% average cost

In view of these assumptions, the cost of maintaining a positive average cash balance is determined by multiplying the average cash balance by the average cost of capital rate.

The Tax Rate

It should be noted that the above cost computation is figured on an after-tax basis. In order to express this cost on a before-tax basis as it will be used in this analysis, the following adjustment can be made:

$$\frac{\text{Average Cash Balance} \times \text{Cost of Capital}}{(1 - \text{Tax Rate})}.$$

Sales

The third independent variable in the analysis is the sales figure. This figure serves the analysis as a proxy variable which measures the transactions needs of the firm. A given level of sales represents the inflows of value earned by the firm. Closely related to this inflow of value are outflows for current assets required to support the sales level. At this level of the analysis it is assumed that all sales and purchases are on a cash basis.

The Indifference Bank Exchange Rate

The dependent variable in this analysis is the indifference bank exchange rate. Considering the average cash balance variable, the financial exchange service offered by the banking system enables the firm to reduce its average cash balance from traditionally maintained levels to a zero average balance. This eliminates for the firm the time cost associated with the investment in cash. The specialized firm's exchange account balance would therefore appear as follows:

Time	*Inflow*	*Outflow*	*Specialized Balance*
1	10	10	0
2		4	–4
3	15	5	6
4		3	3
5		4	–1
6	17	8	8
7		10	–2
8		8	–10
			0

In return for this service, the bank applies the bank exchange rate or discount rate to the firm's sales figure. This rate varies from firm to firm depending upon the needs and risks assumed by the bank. A firm with a stable, predictable pattern of cash inflows and outflows would be charged a lower rate than one whose needs are highly unstable and uncertain.

The *indifference* bank exchange rate is that rate which produces the same total cost under the traditional or self-administered system as the total cost under the centrally administered system. It brings the costs of the two systems to equality. At this exchange rate, and given the figures for the independent variables, the total cost to the firm will be identical regardless of the exchange system employed. The firm is indifferent. Hence, the conclusion may be reached that if the *actual* exchange rate assessed by the bank is lower than the firm's *indifference* exchange rate as computed, it becomes advisable for the firm to adopt the new system.

Factor I: The Average Cash Balance

With the variables thus far introduced it is possible to begin the construction of the indifference model by transforming the cost associated with the traditional average cash balance to an equivalent cost associated with the liquidity provided by the centralized system. Traditionally, the firm administers a cash balance capable of fulfilling its exchange needs. The cost to the firm is the earning requirement of the invested capital.

The firm's alternative to carrying this capital investment is to purchase the service of the exchange function externally from the centrally-administered exchange system. In this case, the fixed capital cost is replaced by a current expense in the form of the bank charge.

The relevant variables described above may be expressed as follows to determine the indifference bank exchange rate:

$$IXR_c \times S \times (1 - TR) = ACB \times CC$$

$$IXR_c = \frac{ACB \times CC}{S\,(1 - TR)}$$

$$IXR_c = \frac{1}{S}\left[\frac{ACB \times CC}{1 - TR}\right]$$

where: IXR_c = Indifference Exchange Rate—cash factor
ACB = Average Cash Balance
CC = Cost of Capital
S = Sales
TR = Tax Rate.

Illustrative Figures Assumed:

Average Cash Balance	$ 30,000
Sales	300,000
Cost of Capital	15%
Tax Rate	50%

IXR_c as computed = 3% (of sales).

Comparison of costs under alternative systems. The self-administered system at the indifference exchange rate level is based on an average cash balance of $30,000. Given the cost of capital requirement of 15 percent, this investment must generate $4,500 in earnings after taxes. This represents the relevant cost to the firm.

The centrally administered system eliminates the need for this fixed asset and related capital cost. Instead, a variable expense is charged amounting to $9,000. The effective cost after tax adjustment is $4,500 determined as follows:

Sales	$300,000
IXR_c	.03
	9,000
Tax Rate	.50
	$4,500

Thus, in either instance, the cost to the firm is $4,500.

Graphic representation of the indifference bank exchange rate. This level of the analysis for determining the indifference bank exchange rate with four independent variables may be shown graphically allowing the values for three of the variables to be shifted. These relationships are shown in Figure 4.

To determine the indifference exchange rate from these graphs, the procedure is to select the average cash balance on the left axis of the upper graph and move laterally to the right to the relevant Cost of Capital level. Directly beneath the intersection of these values on the horizontal axis lies the required Earnings After Taxes. By extending this line downward into the lower graph to the relevant Sales level, and then horizontally to the left axis, the Indifference Bank Exchange Rate adjusted for a 50 percent tax rate is identified. The

Figure 4

THE INDIFFERENCE BANK EXCHANGE RATE CALCULATOR

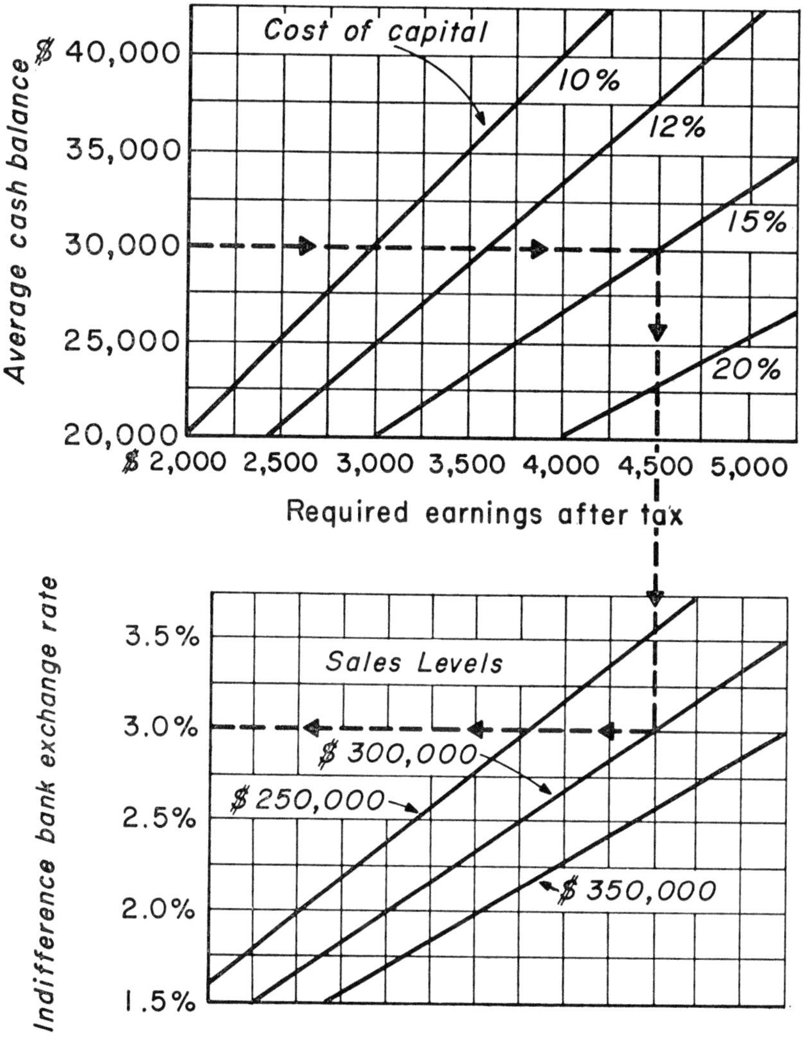

Average cash balance
$ 40,000
35,000
30,000
25,000
20,000
Cost of capital
10%
12%
15%
20%
$ 2,000 2,500 3,000 3,500 4,000 4,500 5,000
Required earnings after tax

Indifference bank exchange rate
3.5%
3.0%
2.5%
2.0%
1.5%
Sales Levels
$ 300,000
$ 250,000
$ 350,000

preceding example using an Average Cash Balance of $30,000, Sales of $300,000, and a Cost of Capital of 15 percent results in an Indifference Exchange Rate of 3.0 percent as was computed numerically.

Given these figures and the related assumptions, the maximum rate which could be paid to the bank for its exchange service is 3 percent of sales. If a higher rate is paid, the firm's financial position would be affected adversely. A lower rate would result in economies for the firm.

The remainder of this chapter further develops the model by introducing deferred payments and charges, variable costs of exchange and credit, and marketable securities. Each variable is introduced separately with its related assumptions until the model is completed containing the variables relevant to the financial exchange decision. The figures used to illustrate each variable are maintained throughout the analysis.

Factor I-A: Marketable Securities and Interest Income

The exchange function of the firm may, in part, be facilitated by holding time deposits or short-term securities in lieu of cash. This enables the firm to transform its liquid resources to alternative sub-uses and thereby reduce carrying costs.

It is assumed that:

1) The average marketable securities balance is maintained for transactions-precautionary purposes related to operating receipts and disbursements as a sub-use of the cash balance.

A centralized system eliminates the need for marketable securities serving the liquidity needs of the business. Again, the extent of cost reduction associated with the elimination of this asset may be charged by the bank without negatively affecting the financial position of the firm. The elimination of interest income has the opposite effect. The indifference cost of these variables is shown as follows:

$$IXR_{ms} \times S \times (1 - TR) = MS \times CC - II \times (1 - TR)$$

$$IXR_{ms} = \frac{MS \times CC}{S\,(1 - TR)} - \frac{II}{S}$$

where: IXR_{ms} = Indifference Exchange Rate–marketable securities

MS = Marketable Securities

II = Interest Income.

When this factor is inserted into the developing model, the expression appears as:

$$IXR_{s1} = \frac{ACB \times CC}{S\,(1 - TR)} + \frac{MS \times CC}{S\,(1 - TR)} - \frac{II}{S}$$

$$IXR_{s1} = \frac{1}{S}\left[\frac{CC\,(ACB + MS)}{1 - TR} - II\right]$$

where: IXR_{s1} = Indifference Bank Exchange Rate—subtotal including cash, marketable sec., and interest income.

Illustrative Figures Assumed:

Average Cash Balance		$ 27,000
Average Marketable Securities		3,000
Sales		300,000
Net Interest Income		100
Cost of Capital		15%
Tax Rate		50%
IXR_{ms} as computed	= .27%	
IXR_c as recomputed	= 2.70	
IXR_{s1} as computed	= 2.97	

Cost comparisons.

Self Administered Firm:

Average Cash Balance	$27,000 × .15 =	$4,050
Marketable Securities	3,000 × .15 =	450
Interest Income	100 × .50 =	−50
		$4,450

Specialized Firm:

Sales	$300,000 × .0297 × .50 =	$4,450

In this situation where a part of the firm's liquidity for transactions-precautionary purposes is in the form of marketable securities, the indifference rate decreases slightly. This decrease reflects the effect of interest income which would be eliminated if the central system were adopted. Hence, in situation *I-A* including marketable securities and interest income, the firm would need to pay a lower exchange rate than in situation *I* where the firm's liquidity is all maintained in the form of cash.

Factor II: Accounts Receivable

A part of the financial exchange function lies in the timing of the transfer of economic value. To aid in the selling of its output, the firm may provide for exchange to be delayed for a period of time by creating the accounts receivable asset. This is a convenience to the buyer. Its cost is measured by applying the firm's cost of capital rate to the average level of the accounts receivable asset.

The centralized system shifts the credit function from the firm to the bank. All sales by the firm are on a cash basis with the banking system acting to effect the immediate transfer of value. If the buyer then wishes to defer payment, he may do so as agreed with the bank by incurring an explicit charge for this convenience.

For the firm to remain indifferent to shifting the credit function from its control to the bank's control, its rate of return on the remaining investment must not be adversely affected. Total cost to the firm under the new system must not exceed the total cost of the traditional system. The indifference cost of the accounts receivable variable is shown as follows:

$$IXR_{ar} \times S \times (1 - TR) = AR \times CC$$

$$IXR_{ar} = \frac{AR \times CC}{S\,(1 - TR)}$$

where: IXR_{ar} = Indifference Exchange Rate–accounts receivable
AR = Accounts Receivable.

With this factor added to the model, it appears as:

$$IXR_{s2} = \frac{ACB \times CC}{S\,(1 - TR)} + \frac{MS \times CC}{S\,(1 - TR)} + \frac{AR \times CC}{S\,(1 - TR)} - \frac{II}{S}$$

$$IXR_{s2} = \frac{1}{S}\left[\frac{CC\,(ACB + MS + AR)}{1 - TR} - II\right]$$

where: IXR_{s2} = Indifference Bank Exchange Rate—subtotal including cash, marketable securities, interest income, and accounts receivable.

Illustrative Figures Assumed:

Average Cash Balance		$27,000
Average Marketable Securities		3,000
Average Accounts Receivable		20,000
Sales		300,000
Net Interest Income		100
Cost of Capital		15%
Tax Rate		50%
IXR_c brought forward	= 2.70%	
IXR_{ms} brought forward	= .27	
IXR_{ar} as computed	= 2.00	
IXR_{s2} as computed	= 4.97	

Cost comparisons.

Self-Administered Firm:

Average Cash Balance	$27,000 × .15 =	$4,050
Marketable Securities	3,000 × .15 =	450
Accounts Receivable	20,000 × .15 =	3,000
Interest Income	100 × .50 =	−50
		$7,450

Specialized Firm:

Sales	$300,000 × .0497 × .50 =	$7,450

Thus, if the firm removes from its control the cash, marketable securities, and accounts receivable variables, it can afford to pay to the bank 4.97 percent of its sales and maintain the earning requirement on its remaining capital sources.

Factors III and IV: Variable Exchange Costs and Variable Credit Costs

The financial exchange function may, in part, be performed by using variable exchange expenses under traditional systems. These costs would be incurred for such items as clerical work for handling receipts and payments, related supplies, and traditional bank service charges. These costs may be shown in terms of the indifference centralized cost as:

$$IXR_{vec} = \frac{VEC}{S}$$

where: IXR_{vec} = Indifference Exchange Rate–variable exchange costs
VEC = Variable Exchange Costs.

In the same manner, variable credit costs also may be incurred by the firm for various purposes such as credit investigation, collection, bad debts, and clerical work. These costs would be eliminated under the central exchange system and replaced by the bank rate charged to the firm. The cost may be expressed as:

$$IXR_{vcc} = \frac{VCC}{S}$$

where: IXR_{vcc} = Indifference Exchange Rate–variable credit costs
VCC = Variable Credit Costs.

These two factors may be added to the model as follows:

$$IXR_{s3} = \frac{ACB \times CC}{S\,(1-TR)} + \frac{MS \times CC}{S\,(1-TR)} + \frac{AR \times CC}{S\,(1-TR)} + \frac{VEC}{S} + \frac{VCC}{S} - \frac{II}{S}$$

$$IXR_{s3} = \frac{1}{S}\left[\frac{CC\,(ACB + MS + AR)}{1-TR} + VEC + VCC - II\right]$$

where: IXR_{s3} = Indifference Bank Exchange Rate–subtotal including cash, marketable securities, interest income, accounts receivable, variable exchange costs, and variable credit costs.

Illustrative Figures Assumed:

Average Cash Balance	$27,000
Average Marketable Securities	3,000
Average Accounts Receivable	20,000
Sales	300,000
Net Interest Income	100
Variable Exchange Costs	1,500
Variable Credit Costs	2,500
Cost of Capital	15%
Tax Rate	50%

IXR_c	brought forward	= 2.70%
IXR_{ms}	brought forward	= .27
IXR_{ar}	as computed	= 2.00
IXR_{vec}	as computed	= .50
IXR_{vcc}	as computed	= .83
IXR_{s3}	as computed	= 6.30

Cost comparisons.

Self-Administered Firm:

Average Cash Balance	$27,000 × .15 =	$4,050
Marketable Securities	3,000 × .15 =	450
Accounts Receivable	20,000 × .15 =	3,000
Interest Income	100 × .50 =	−50
Variable Exchange Costs	1,500 × .50 =	750
Variable Credit Costs	2,500 × .50 =	1,250
		$9,450

Specialized Firm:

Sales	$300,000 × .0630 × .50 = $9,450

This concludes the cost transformations of the assets and variable costs affected by the change over to a central exchange system.

Sources of Funds: Payables vs. Bank Credit

Under present practice, principal sources of funds for financing current assets are trade credit and other current payables. These accounts represent to the firm the drawing of economic resources within its control. Together with this drawing comes the obligation for compensating these sources of capital. This compensation can appear in several forms. Accounts payable, for example, carry financial exchange costs in three categories: hidden costs, lost discounts, and explicit interest charges.

Hidden costs of trade credit are included in the purchase price of the goods. Although a selling agreement may state settlement terms as "30 days cash," indicating that there is no credit charge for 30 days borrowing, the seller must cover these time costs of capital. To do this, some part of the purchase price of the goods represents a return for the borrowing of these funds for the 30 day period. Thus, the hidden credit cost.

Lost discounts represent a second method for recovering time costs of capital. If terms are stated as "2/10; n/30" for example, 2 percent of the purchase price is set aside for the convenience of deferring payment for an additional 20 days. Annualized, this cost equals 36 percent, which is equal to the before-tax return required by a firm with a cost of capital of 18 percent and a tax rate of 50 percent.

Finally, credit costs may be assessed explicitly by extending the terms in the above example to "2/10; n/30"; 12 percent. In this case, if the purchaser wishes to further delay his payment, he does so at an explicitly stated cost.

Other current liabilities as well should be viewed as being accompanied by costs. In most cases these are not explicitly stated and are hidden in operating accounts when, in fact, they should be separated out and categorized as costs of financial exchange. Taxes payable, as an example, are not accompanied by an explicit interest charge. Yet, due to the fact that the governmental agencies involved must wait until specified dates to receive amounts due, some cost should be recognized. If it were possible to pay the tax as it was incurred, these agencies would receive the funds sooner and therefore would require a smaller amount. The difference in amounts should be considered as an item in the cost of capital computations.

Similarly, wages payable representing a one or two week gap between services received and settlement carry an imputed cost. Theoretically, a slightly higher wage must be paid if a delay in payment is expected by the employee. This increase is a measurement of the cost of financial exchange and, again, should be classified apart from operating expenses for services received.

Hidden costs such as have been described should, therefore, be recognized in the average cost of capital computation. Even though they are not explicitly stated, they are present and have an effect on the capital structure and related risk. No source of capital is costless or riskless.

Central Exchange System

A central exchange system eliminates the costs of trade credit and other payables. Businesses no longer offer as a part of their product package the convenience of deferred payments. As a result, the selling price of the goods should be a cash price covering only product costs and related capital costs. The seller receives immediately this cash price from the bank. The buyer then makes the choice as to whether or not he wishes to obtain credit from the bank to settle the obligation, or to settle immediately from other sources.

Bank credit arises when the buyer maintains a negative average balance in his bank exchange account. For a period of time the average of the inflows and outflows may be negative. Thus, bank credit is created and must be paid for with explicitly stated interest charges. The negative average cash balance is illustrated below.

Time	*Inflows*	*Outflows*	*Self-Sufficient Balance*
1	5	10	–5
2		4	–9
3	15	5	1
4		3	–2
5		4	–6
6	17	8	3
7		10	–7
8		8	–15
			–40 ÷ 8 = –5

The maintenance of a negative balance represents the usual leverage decision associated with the use of short-term credit in the capital structure.

The activity account. The maintenance of a negative position with the central system indicates the use of banking funds for two separate, but related aspects of financial exchange. First, the negative balance itself represents the continued use of short-term credit. The level of this credit would be a subject for negotiation with the banking system. In this theoretical discussion, it has been assumed that this level is such that the firm's debt:equity ratio remains unchanged.

The second aspect of the firm's use of bank funds centers around the daily inflows and outflows of funds for the purposes of operating transactions. This exchange activity was described earlier in the discussion of movements around a zero balance for which no interest charge is assessed. Rather, the exchange service fee is the means used for compensating the banking system.

To distinguish between these two uses of the bank's resources, the firm's exchange account is divided into two sections. The first contains the level of continuing bank credit agreed upon. The second part described as the Activity Account contains the daily inflows and outflows of values related to operations. As long as this account maintains an average balance of zero, no added charges are assessed. If a negative balance is maintained, then interest is charged and a review of the firm's use of bank credit would be indicated with the intention of either permanently increasing the credit portion of the account, or securing funds from other sources to liquidate the added borrowing.

If the activity account maintained an average positive balance, interest would be applied to offset the interest expense on the permanent level of borrowing.

In this discussion it is assumed that:

1) Current liabilities will be converted to an amount of bank credit when the centralized system is adopted which maintains the firm's traditional debt:equity ratio. By maintaining this proportion, the effect of financial leverage is held constant.
2) The cost of bank credit obtained from the central system is equal to the cost of the present sources of short-term funds.

Concerning the first assumption, it should be noted that since the removal of financial exchange assets results in a contraction of total assets, funds are also eliminated. On the funds side, this reduction is applied proportionally, thereby shrinking each source in such a way as to leave the debt:equity ratio constant and the effect of financial leverage unchanged. It can be seen that with this proportional shrink, assuming a constant cost for short-term sources, the average cost of capital remains unchanged. In the following illustration, $50,000 of assets have been eliminated:

Source	*Amount*	*Percent of Total*	*Cost*	*Index*
Current Liab.	$8,750	12.5%	8%	100
Equity	61,250	87.5	16	1,400
		100.0%		1,500

1,500 ÷ 100% = 15% average cost.

Factor V: Payables

If the cost of the present form of payables is equal to the cost of short-term credit under the central exchange system, and the proportional level of the obligation remains constant, the indifference bank exchange rate will not be affected. The cost of this source of funds replaces the costs of the present sources. Under the central exchange system, this cost would simply be substituted for present costs, thus leaving the average cost of capital rate unaffected.

As a practical matter, it is unlikely that there would be an immediate adjustment in prices for separating out and removing credit costs to arrive at "cash" values. Such adjustments would eventually be forced by competitive pressures requiring a relatively long period of time. Nevertheless, if an explicit bank interest charge would appear, this would result in an additional cost rather than a substituted cost. Therefore, when the net amount of these costs increases as a result of the new system, the firm must pay a lower exchange rate in order to leave its total financial position unaffected. Should the net cost happen to be lower resulting from the efficiencies gained by the new system, the indifference rate would be increased. The cost of these variables is expressed in an indifference rate as follows:

$$IXR_{bc} = \frac{J}{S}$$

where: IXR_{bc} = Indifference Exchange Rate—short-term bank credit

J = Net cost or net saving of changing from payables to bank credit. This figure may be positive or negative.

The indifference cost of this factor may be computed in the following manner:

Illustrative Figures Assumed:	
Hidden cost of payables	$ 1,800
Discounts lost	200
Interest charges	400
Actual reduction expected	600
The value of J therefore follows:	
Theoretical reductions in cost	$−2,400
Actual reduction	+600
Additional cost − (J)	$−1,800

$$IXR_{bc} = \frac{\$\text{-}1{,}800}{300{,}000}$$

$$IXR_{bc} = -.6\%.$$

If the value for J had been positive, the IXR_{bc} would have been added to the total IXR rate. This factor will be included in the total model and cost comparisons in a later section.

Revenue Adjustments

The final factors to be included in the model concern adjustments in revenue arising from the removal of the credit function from the firm's control. Such adjustments have two effects on the firm's indifference bank exchange rate. First, if revenue changes as the result of the new exchange system being adopted, the loss or benefit should be included in the model. Second, a change in revenue affects the arithmetic computation of the indifference exchange rate. Each of these effects will be discussed in turn.

Factor VI: Profit

A primary concern of many potential users of the centralized exchange system is the likely change in sales which could occur. For a firm which relies on the credit function to attract and retain customers, the removal of this competitive tool could result in lost sales. Retail firms, for example, which have highly developed charge-a-plate systems are particularly concerned about potential losses.

At the other extreme, firms traditionally unable to extend credit will now face the possibility of increasing sales due to the availability of credit through the banking system. In either of these cases, the effect of such a change in revenue should be considered in the indifference decision. The firm which expects losses to occur would be able to pay a lower indifference rate, while the firm expecting gains could afford a higher rate.

A second adjustment which should be recognized is the possible selling price reduction associated with the elimination of the accounts receivable asset and related capital cost. If pure competition is present, the firm's selling price includes a charge for credit. When the credit function is no longer controlled by the firm, it should reduce its selling price by the amount of the accounts receivable capital cost. This price reduction would be received by the buyer, who would then redirect it to the bank in return for bank credit. If the firm does not make such price reductions, theoretical propositions state that it would be driven out of existence due to competitive pressures.

Since pure competition cannot be assumed to describe practical business conditions, price reductions may not be granted. However, in the event that they are granted, this reduction should be recognized in the model. The extent of these reductions causes the indifference rate to be reduced by an equal amount.

The net cost of these two possibilities for revenue adjustments will be added to the model in the K variable expressed as:

$$IXR_k = \frac{K}{S}$$

where: IXR_k = Indifference Exchange Rate–revenue adjustments

K = Gain or loss of profit due to change in unit sales or change in selling price per unit. This figure may be positive or negative.

The value of K may be computed as:

Theoretical reduction in selling price to remove capital costs of

$$\text{Accounts Receivable} = \frac{AR \times CC}{1 - TR} = \$6{,}000$$

Estimated actual reduction in selling price		$ 2,000
Estimated loss in unit sales = 5%		
Reduction in revenue	$15,000	
Reduction in cost of goods	–7,500	
Reduction in other expenses	–500	
Reduction in net income before tax	$ 7,000	7,000
		$–9,000

$$IRX_k = -3.00\%.$$

Cost comparisons.

Self-Administered Firm:

Reduction in Profit $\$9{,}000 \times .50 = \$4{,}500$

Specialized Firm:

Sales $\$300{,}000 \times .03 \times .50 = \$4{,}500$

Since this factor represents losses resulting from the adoption of the central system, the 3 percent must be subtracted from the total indifference rate to recognize a reduction in the amount that the firm can afford to pay to the bank for the new service. If sales were expected to increase as a result of the new system, the *K* factor would be added in the total computation.

Factor VII: Revenue Changes and the Exchange Rate Computation

At the indifference point where the indifference exchange rate and the actual bank exchange rate are equal, the dollar cost to the firm and the dollar revenue earned by the bank are identical. The bank's objective is to recover this amount from the firm to cover the costs of the exchange system. As a practical matter, the bank has the problem of communicating the amount of this cost to the firm. In this study, the cost is communicated to the firm as a bank exchange rate geared to the firm's sales figure. This method has been chosen due to its ease of implementation and the observable fact that it is employed by existing bank card plans.

The indifference cost of the factors computed to this point has been based on *unadjusted* sales figures. If the bank were now to use *adjusted* figures recognizing changes in sales resulting from the adoption of the new system for the rate computations, it would always obtain a rate higher than the firm's rate and the system would therefore never be adopted. Hence, a final factor must be introduced to avoid this inconsistency. It is expressed as:

$$IXR' = \frac{S}{S_e} \times IXR_s$$

where: S = Unadjusted Sales

S_e = Sales adjusted for expected changes

IXR_s = The Unadjusted Indifference Rate

IXR' = The Indifference Rate adjusted for revenue changes.

Computation of Factor VII. Sales at the present level have been assumed to be \$300,000. Expected sales adjustments associated with the K factor discussed above are \$17,000. Hence, the expected sales figure which will be used as a basis for the bank charge will be \$283,000. This results in a factor of:

$$\frac{\$300{,}000}{283{,}000} = 1.06$$

$$IXR' = 1.06 \times IXR_s\,.$$

The Completed Indifference Bank Exchange Rate Model

The completed model may now be presented together with data demonstrating the cost transformations at the indifference bank exchange rate. The incomplete financial statements of the self-sufficient company and the specializing company presented at the beginning of this chapter will now be completed to include illustrative values for the accounts. These are shown in Figures 5 and 6. Proof of the equality of costs at the indifference point as computed will also be presented.

Figure 5

COMPLETED STATEMENTS FOR SELF-SUFFICIENT COMPANY

Balance Sheet
Self-Sufficient Company

Cash	$ 27,000	Current Payables	$ 15,000
Marketable Securities	3,000	Other Sources	105,000
Accounts Receivable	20,000		
Inventory	30,000		
Fixed Assets	40,000		
	$120,000		$120,000

Income Statement
Self-Sufficient Company

Sales		$300,000
Cost of Goods Sold		150,000
Gross Profit		$150,000
Expenses:		
Wages	$80,000	
Selling	20,000	
Administrative	10,000	
Bank Expense	600	
Credit Department	1,000	
Bad Debts	1,500	
Cashiers Expense	900	
Discounts Lost	200	
Other Expense	1,900	
Total Expenses		116,100
Net Operating Income		33,900
Interest Income		100
Interest Expense		—400
Net Income Before Tax		33,600
Income Taxes		16,800
Net Income		$ 16,800

Figure 6

COMPLETED STATEMENTS FOR SPECIALIZED COMPANY

Balance Sheet
Specialized Company

Inventory	$ 30,000	Bank Credit	$ 8,750
Fixed Assets	40,000	Other Sources	61,250
	$ 70,000		$ 70,000

Income Statement
Specialized Company

Sales		$283,000
Cost of Goods Sold		142,500
Gross Profit		140,500
Expenses:		
Wages	$79,700	
Selling	19,800	
Administrative	10,000	
Bank Exchange	8,100	
Bank Interest	1,400	
Other Expense	1,900	
Total Expenses		120,900
Net Income Before Taxes		19,600
Income Taxes		9,800
Net Income		$ 9,800

The Model and Variables

Factor: VII I I-A II III

$$IXR' = \frac{S}{S_e}\left|\frac{ACB \times CC}{S\,(1-TR)} + \frac{MS \times CC}{S\,(1-TR)} + \frac{AR \times CC}{S\,(1-TR)} + \frac{VEC}{S}\right.$$

IV I-A V VI

$$\left. + \frac{VCC}{S} - \frac{II}{S} + \frac{J}{S} + \frac{K}{S}\right|$$

$$IXR' = \frac{1}{S_e}\left| \frac{CC\ (ACB + MS + AR)}{1 - TR} + VEC + VCC - II + J + K \right|$$

where: IXR' = Indifference Bank Exchange Rate
ACB = Average Cash Balance
MS = Marketable Securities
AR = Accounts Receivable
CC = Cost of Capital Rate
VEC = Variable Exchange Costs
VCC = Variable Credit Costs
II = Interest Income
TR = Tax Rate
J = Net savings or net cost of changing from trade credit to bank credit
K = Gain or loss of profit due to change in unit sales or change in selling price per unit
S = Unadjusted Sales
S_e = Sales adjusted for expected changes of K.

The total indifference bank exchange rate as computed by applying the completed model to these data is 2.86 percent of sales. This same rate may be obtained by combining the rates previously computed for the individual factors.

$$
\begin{aligned}
IXR_c &= 2.70\% \\
IXR_{ms} &= .27 \\
IXR_{ar} &= 2.00 \\
IXR_{vec} &= .50 \\
IXR_{vcc} &= .83 \\
IXR_{bc} &= -.60 \\
IXR_k &= -3.00 \\
\hline
IXR_s &= 2.70 \\
\frac{S}{S_e} &= \times\ 1.06 \\
\hline
IXR' &= 2.86\%.
\end{aligned}
$$

Cost comparisons.

Self-Sufficient Firm:		
Average Cash Balance	$27,000 × .15 =	$ 4,050
Marketable Securities	3,000 × .15 =	450
Accounts Receivable	20,000 × .15 =	3,000
Reduction in Payables	$15,000 – $ 8,750 × .08 =	–500
Cost of Goods Sold:		
Purchase Price Reductions	0	
Unit Sale Reductions	$ 7,500	
Other Expenses:		
Wages	300	
Selling	200	
Bank Expense	600	
Credit Department	1,000	
Bad Debts	1,500	
Cashiers Expense	900	
Discounts Lost	200	
Interest Expense	400	
Total Eliminated Expenses	12,600 × .50 =	6,300
Total Eliminated Cost		$13,300
Eliminated Revenue:		
Selling Price Reductions	$ 2,000	
Loss in Unit Sales	15,000	
Interest Income	100	
Total Eliminated Revenue	$17,100 × .50 =	–8,550
Net Eliminated Costs of Financial Exchange		$ 4,750
Specialized Firm:		
Bank Exchange Expense	$ 8,100 × .50 =	$ 4,050
Bank Interest Expense	1,400 × .50 =	700
Total Added Costs of Financial Exchange		$ 4,750

Rate of Return on Other Sources of Capital

The final measurement of the equality of the two systems at the indifference bank exchange rate level lies in the rate of return on long-term sources of capital. In the examples presented, long-term sources are assumed to have a cost of 16 percent after taxes. Under the centrally-administered system, long-term sources amounted to $105,000. When related to the net profit after taxes figure of $16,800, a rate of return of 16 percent is obtained.

The centrally-administered exchange system eliminates cash, marketable securities, and accounts receivable and the related financing. Thus, long-term sources of capital are shrunk proportionally to $61,250. Net income after taxes is reflected as $9,800. Again, this represents a rate of return of 16 percent on the capital investment.

Partially Adopted or Dual Systems

As the centralized system moves closer to becoming an operational reality, it is likely that it will be adopted gradually rather than as an abrupt, complete shift. A gradual change-over implies the need for the firm to maintain dual systems of exchange until the transition becomes complete. To recognize this problem, the variables in the analysis may be changed from "totals" of each item to the "eliminatable" portion of each item. Thus, if all accounts receivable, for example, were not taken over by the bank, only the eliminatable accounts or those wishing to use bank credit rather than trade credit would be inserted into the model. By identifying these eliminatable items, the analysis would determine the indifference bank exchange rate needed to equate the total costs being incurred for these items.

It is also probable that the firm may be able to gain economies in the exchange function by adopting only individual segments of the centralized service and retaining traditional methods for the balance of the variables. For example, a firm may wish to adopt the services related to the cash balance and marketable securities decision, but retain the credit operation. To evaluate this decision, the indifference rates for the individually related factors may be used. From a marginal analysis standpoint, as an additional factor is added to the analysis, the incremental cost and benefit may be considered to determine the extent to which the new services may be adopted profitably.

Conclusion

In this chapter the variables which will be affected by the introduction of a centralized financial exchange system have been identified and transformed into cost data which can be used to evaluate the desirability of adopting the new system. As presented, however, the model assumes static data or "best estimates" of data which can be used to compute a single indifference exchange rate. Although such an approach is typical of many business decisions, the quality of such decisions may be improved if added information is supplied concerning the uncertainty associated with the data inputs and computations. In Chapter V, a method for handling uncertainty will be introduced to complement the indifference exchange rate model and increase its usefulness.

V

Introduction of Uncertainty

The model thus far developed identifies and relates the variables relevant to the financial exchange decision under conditions of certainty and perfect information. Realistically, however, the usefulness of the model would be limited if accommodation were not made for the dynamics of the uncertainty associated with practical business conditions. Perfect information does not exist. Even "best estimates" and averages for the variables can lead to erroneous decisions. Using such data to compute a single indifference exchange rate does not communicate complete decision information when uncertainty exists, since this implies that to result in the predicted *IXR*, each of the variables, too, must occur as predicted. Such accuracy is seldom achieved.

To increase the usefulness of the indifference exchange rate model, a method for handling uncertainty is needed. It is the purpose of this chapter to introduce such a method to the immediate problem of the financial exchange decision. A simulated problem will be presented to illustrate the application of the method and the intended use of its results.

Methodology

To communicate to the decision maker the amount of uncertainty that is associated with the computation of an indifference exchange rate, a probabilistic dimension may be added to the model. This approach poses that probability distributions be determined for each variable in the model. By applying these determinations, a probability distribution of indifference rates is supplied and may be evaluated in terms of the risk preferences of the decision maker. He may then compare this distribution of rates and the related probabilities with the *actual* service rates offered by the banking system to evaluate the advisability of accepting extended banking services of the kinds discussed in earlier chapters.

The objective of such an approach has been stated by one author as follows:

Since every one of the many factors that enter into the evaluation of a specific decision is subject to some uncertainty, the executive needs a helpful portrayal of the effects that the uncertainty surrounding each of the significant factors has on the returns he is likely to achieve. . . . The method . . . developed combines the variabilities inherent in all the relevant factors. Our objective is to give a clear picture of the relative risk and the probable odds of coming out ahead or behind in light of uncertain foreknowledge.[1]

To accomplish this objective, a system of subjective probabilities can be applied. Such an approach to business problems has been advocated by Schlaifer.[2] According to him, subjective probability theory rests on the following reasoning:

. . . the theory of probability is simply a set of logical deductions from certain basic axioms; the axioms of this particular theory are the following:

1) A probability is a number between 0 and 1 assigned to an event.

2) The sum of the probabilities assigned to a set of mutually exclusive and collectively exhaustive events must be 1.

3) The probability of an event which is composed of a group of mutually exclusive events is the sum of their probabilities.

We are justified in using the theory of probability to calculate "weights" . . . because we have agreed to assign weights in accordance with these three axioms; the axioms are simply our three "basic rules" for assigning weights presented in slightly different language. . . . Henceforth we shall use the word *probability* in exactly the same sense that we have hitherto used the word "weight."

. . . the meaning of "weight" or probability . . . is necessarily an expression of a personal judgment and is therefore necessarily *subjective* in the sense that two reasonable men may assign different probabilities to the same event. This by no means implies, however, that a reasonable man will assign probabilities *arbitrarily*.

Reasonable men base the probabilities which they assign to events in the real world on their experience with events in the real world, and when two reasonable men have had roughly the same experience with a certain kind of event they assign it roughly the same probability.

To apply probability theory to the immediate problem, three specific steps are followed.[3]

1) For *each* of the variables in the analysis, estimates of the range of values for the variable are obtained and probabilities are associated with each value in this range. The average cash balance, for example, may be estimated to range from $17,500 to $42,500 with a most likely value of $30,000. The distribution might appear as follows:

Range of Values ACB Range	*Discrete Values ACB*	*Probability of Occurrence P(ACB)*
$17,500-$22,499	$20,000	.05
22,500- 27,499	25,000	.15
27,500- 32,499	30,000	.60
32,500- 37,499	35,000	.15
37,500- 42,500	40,000	.05
		1.00

It should be noted that the total of the probabilities in the distribution is 1.00. This range of values and related probabilities could be determined subjectively by obtaining estimates from knowledgeable individuals. These estimates would result from the combining of historical data and judgment associated with the variable under consideration.

It should be noted that although Schlaifer describes this method of assigning probabilities as subjective, various amounts of objective information may be involved in addition to experience. Subjective does not mean unfounded feelings, but rather deliberate estimates based on meaningful objective experience and varying amounts of historical information.

2) Select any discrete value and related probability for each of the variables in the indifference exchange rate model and compute

the *IXR*.[4] By multiplying, obtain the product of their related probabilities as follows:

$$P(IXR_x) = P(A)\ P(B) \ldots P(N)$$

where: $P(A) \ldots P(N)$ = Probabilities of each of the specific values of the independent variables used

$P(IXR_x)$ = Probability of the *IXR* resulting from the specific values of the independent variables used.[5]

3) Repeat step two until all possible combinations of the values of the several independent variables have been considered and the related *IXR* probabilities have been computed. Arrange the *IXR* results in descending order with their related probabilities and prepare a cumulative probability distribution.

Expected Results

Using "best estimates" or average data for the variables in the model as developed in Chapter IV would result in one value for the *IXR*. In the example presented in Chapter IV, this rate was 2.86 percent. The decision maker would then compare this rate with the *actual* rate offered by the banking system and accept the centralized service if the indifference rate was higher than the actual rate.

The application of probabilities to the model will result in added information for the decision maker and may lead to a different decision. The results of this procedure might appear as follows:

IXR Distribution	*Probability*	*Cumulative Probability*
1%	.03	.03
2	.05	.08
3	.15	.23
4	.40	.63
5	.20	.83
6	.10	.93
7	.07	1.00

Thus if the actual exchange rate offered to the firm by the bank is 4 percent of sales, the decision maker could relate this to the information by the probability computations

$$\text{Actual Rate} = 4\%$$
$$P(IXR \leq 4\%) = .63.$$

At the 4 percent *IXR* level indications are that there is a 63 percent likelihood that the cost associated with the traditional exchange system will *not* exceed 4 percent of sales. Thus, if the bank charges 4 percent of sales for providing the services, the chances are about two out of three that the firm could perform the service itself for an equivalent or lesser amount. In only 37 percent of the occurrences could the firm reduce costs by adopting the new system. The decision maker would therefore find it advisable to reject the new system unless he prefers high risk situations and chooses to "bet" on obtaining one of the 37 chances.

Illustrative Problem

To illustrate the application of probabilities to the financial exchange decision, an abbreviated sample problem will be presented using only Factor I and related data from the indifference model presented in Chapter IV. Under conditions of certainty, the model would produce the following information:

$$IXR_c = \frac{ACB \times CC}{S(1 - TR)}$$

where: IXR_c = Indifference Exchange Rate—cash factor
ACB = Average Cash Balance
CC = Cost of Capital
S = Sales
TR = Tax Rate.

Best estimates of values for these variables are:

Average Cash Balance	$ 30,000
Sales	300,000
Cost of Capital	15%
Tax Rate	50%
Indifference Exchange Rate =	3%.

Probability Application: Step I, Distributions

Through interviewing procedures and the use of historical data and forecasting, probability distributions for the variables would be determined. The number of intervals in this example is limited to three. This is done for illustrative purposes allowing for manual computations. As the number of variables and the number of intervals for each variable increase, there is a geometric increase in the required number of computations. The actual application of this procedure would require a computer program to perform the computations.

Sales	*(S)*	*P(S)*
$150,000-$249,999	$200,000	.1
250,000- 349,999	300,000	.8
350,000- 450,000	400,000	.1
Cost of Capital	*(CC)*	*P(CC)*
.08 - .12	.10	.2
.13 - .16	.15	.5
.17 - .20	.18	.3
Tax Rate	*(TR)*	*P(TR)*[6]
.50	.50	1.00

Average cash balance. Since there is some degree of *dependency* between the average cash balance and the sales variable, separate estimates of probabilities must be determined for the average cash balance variable as it would relate to each sales level. Thus, given a sales level of $400,000, what would be the probability distribution for the average cash balance variable? How would it perform if sales were $300,000? These distributions might appear as follows:

Interval	*ACB*	*P(ACB| S $400,000)*	*P(ACB| S $300,000)*	*P(ACB| S $200,000)*
$15,000-$24,499	$20,000	.1	.2	.5
25,000- 34,499	30,000	.3	.6	.4
35,000- 45,000	40,000	.6	.2	.1

If there is independence among the variables, one probability distribution is sufficient. Dependence or independence may again be determined subjectively.

Step II, Computation

The IXR_c and related probability of occurrence may be computed for one set of values, c', as follows:[7]

$$IXR_{c'} = \frac{\$30{,}000 \times .15}{\$300{,}000 \times (1 - .5)}$$

$$IXR_{c'} = 3\%$$

$$P(IXR_{c'}) = P(S) \times P(CC) \times P(ACB \mid S\ \$300{,}000)$$

$$P(IXR_{c'}) = .8 \times .5 \times .6$$

$$P(IXR_{c'}) = .24\,.$$

Step III, Cumulative Probability Distribution

The possible combinations of all values for the variables are enumerated in Table 1. A relisting of the IXR results, related probabilities, and cumulative probabilities appears in Table 2.

Table 1

COMBINATIONS OF VARIABLES AND RELATED PROBABILITIES

Sales	*P(S)*	*CC*	*P(CC)*	*ACB*	*P(ACB)*	$IXR_{c'}$[a]	$P(IXR_{c'})$
$400,000	.1	.18	.3	$40,000	.6	3.60%	.018
400,000	.1	.18	.3	30,000	.3	2.70	.009
400,000	.1	.18	.3	20,000	.1	1.80	.003
400,000	.1	.15	.5	40,000	.6	3.00	.030
400,000	.1	.15	.5	30,000	.3	2.25	.015
400,000	.1	.15	.5	20,000	.1	1.50	.005
400,000	.1	.10	.2	40,000	.6	2.00	.012
400,000	.1	.10	.2	30,000	.3	1.50	.006
400,000	.1	.10	.2	20,000	.1	1.00	.002
300,000	.8	.18	.3	40,000	.2	4.80	.048
300,000	.8	.18	.3	30,000	.6	3.60	.144
300,000	.8	.18	.3	20,000	.2	2.40	.048
300,000	.8	.15	.5	40,000	.2	4.00	.080
300,000	.8	.15	.5	30,000	.6	3.00	.240
300,000	.8	.15	.5	20,000	.2	2.00	.080
300,000	.8	.10	.2	40,000	.2	2.66	.032
300,000	.8	.10	.2	30,000	.6	2.00	.096
300,000	.8	.10	.2	20,000	.2	1.33	.032
200,000	.1	.18	.3	40,000	.1	7.20	.003
200,000	.1	.18	.3	30,000	.4	5.40	.012
200,000	.1	.18	.3	20,000	.5	3.60	.015
200,000	.1	.15	.5	40,000	.1	6.00	.005
200,000	.1	.15	.5	30,000	.4	4.50	.020
200,000	.1	.15	.5	20,000	.5	3.00	.025
200,000	.1	.10	.2	40,000	.1	4.00	.002
200,000	.1	.10	.2	30,000	.4	3.00	.008
200,000	.1	.10	.2	20,000	.5	2.00	.010

[a]The computation of the IXR contains an adjustment for the tax rate of 50 percent.

Table 2

DISTRIBUTION OF *IXR* VALUES, RELATED PROBABILITIES, AND CUMULATIVE PROBABILITIES

$IXR_{c'}$	$P(IXR_{c'})$	$P(IXR_c)$	*Cumulative* $P(IXR_c)$
1.00	.002	.002	.002
1.33	.032	.032	.034
1.50	.006		
1.50	.005	.011	.045
1.80	.003	.003	.048
2.00	.012		
2.00	.080		
2.00	.096		
2.00	.010	.198	.246
2.25	.015	.015	.261
2.40	.048	.048	.309
2.66	.032	.032	.341
2.70	.009	.009	.350
3.00	.240		
3.00	.030		
3.00	.008		
3.00	.025	.303	.653
3.60	.144		
3.60	.018		
3.60	.015	.177	.830
4.00	.080		
4.00	.002	.082	.912
4.50	.020	.020	.932
4.80	.048	.048	.980
5.40	.012	.012	.992
6.00	.005	.005	.997
7.20	.003	.003	1.000
	1.000	1.000	

The Decision Graph

The information obtained from the probability computations may be summarized and interpreted in graphic form as portrayed by the ogive graph in Figure 7. This graph shows the array of indifference exchange rates and related cumulative probabilities for the set of data assumed in the illustrative problems. The axes are labeled accordingly with cumulative probabilities on the y axis and the indifference exchange rates on the x axis.

To interpret the graph, the axes may be labeled alternatively as the actual exchange rates offered by the banking system on the x axis, and the chances that the deciding firm's costs of maintaining its tra-

Figure 7

The Decision Graph

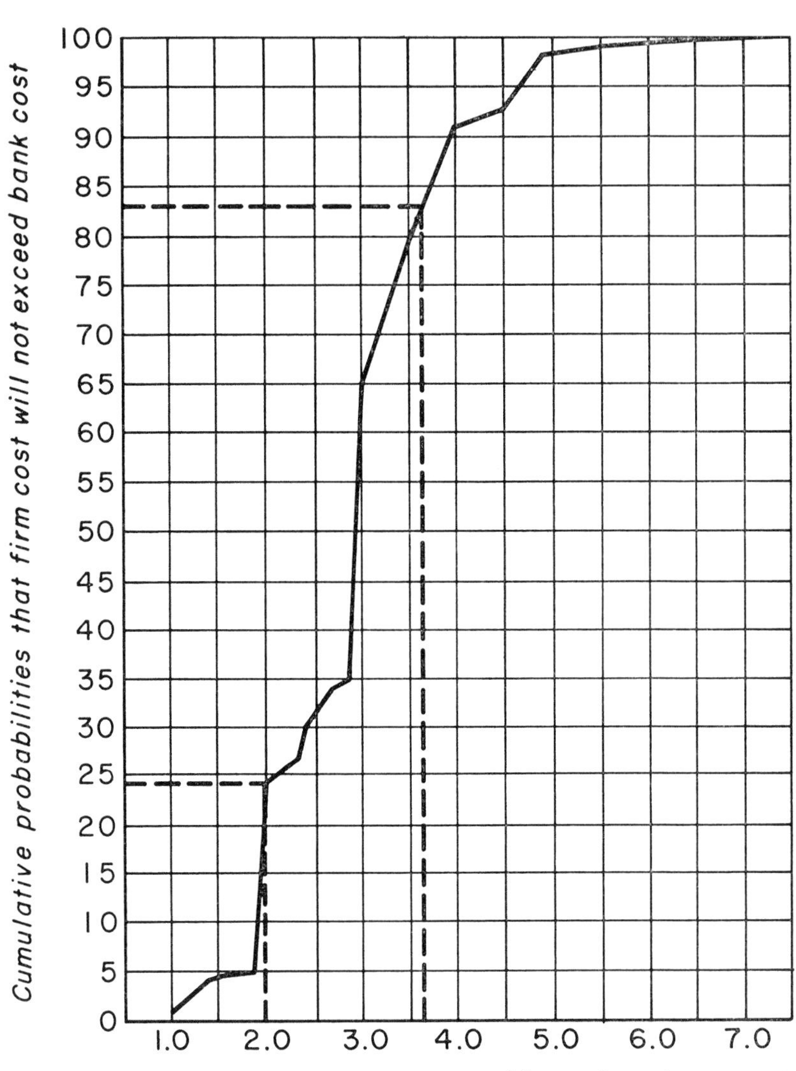

ditional system will not exceed the costs offered by the bank on the y axis. If, for example, the actual rate offered by the bank were 3.6 percent, the graph indicates that there is an 83 percent chance that the firm's traditional cost would not exceed the charges of the bank. Hence, the conclusion would be reached that in 83 of 100 occurrences the firm will minimize costs by maintaining its traditional system. In only 17 of 100 occurrences would there be a saving if the new system were adopted.

Alternatively, if the actual rate offered by the bank were 2 percent, there is about a 25 percent chance that the firm's cost would not exceed the bank's cost. Accordingly, it would be advisable for the firm to adopt the new system.

Thus the addition of the probability dimension to the model provides increased information concerning the *IXR* decision. It may be noted that without the probability information applied to the computation of the *IXR* for the cash balance factor, the rate was 3 percent. With the addition of probabilities, it can be seen from Table 2 and the graph that at the 3 percent level, there is a 65 percent chance that the firm's cost will not exceed the bank cost. In 65 of 100 chances, the firm will actually minimize costs by maintaining its traditional system. It is therefore demonstrated that the application of probabilities can lead to decisions which are different from those reached using best estimates and median values for the factors being considered.

Conclusion

In Chapters IV and V a method has been presented which will enable the individual firm to evaluate the cost and uncertainty associated with the financial exchange decision. By computing its indifference bank exchange rate and the associated probability distribution, the firm has the information necessary to determine the effect on its financial position of adopting the centralized system to be offered by the banking community. From the bank's standpoint, the indifference rate information sets an upper limit on the actual charge that can be assessed to obtain a favorable response from its potential buyers of the service. It is hoped that the ability to obtain this information will aid the parties involved to achieve new levels of private and social efficiencies.

VI

Application of the Model: A Case Study

The nature of the financial exchange function has attributes which are common to all businesses. Firms must exhibit some form of liquidity which enables them to interact with each other and thereby obtain, process, and disperse resources related to their primary productive activities. Values flow continually through the various stages of the production cycle leading to value added. In the preceding chapters these attributes of exchange systems and a method for evaluating related costs have been discussed from a generalized perspective. Theoretical, abstract relationships have been presented.

In order to begin the bridge from abstraction to implementation, a study of an individual, on-going firm has been undertaken. It was the intention of this study to apply the indifference model and the concepts of an integrated financial exchange system to a practical situation, thereby leading to a better understanding of their capabilities and limitations. The results of the case study are presented in this chapter.

Profile of the Company

Cooperation for participation in this study was offered by the owner and president of a small business incorporated in Michigan with annual sales of approximately $640,000. The company is in the elevator maintenance service business and employs 40 individuals. Hereafter, the subject firm will be referred to as the "company."

Approximately 40 percent of the total sales of the company are derived from "full maintenance contract" service extended at present to some 250 customers involving 600 elevators. Each of these customers enters into a contract with the company for full maintenance which guarantees the provision of specified services and specified parts necessary to maintain the elevator in normal working condition. Typically, the contract holder pays a fixed monthly rate to the company for this service ranging from $35 to $190.

In addition to the full service contracts, some 20 percent of total sales is comprised of partial service contracts. These contracts generally include inspection, oil, and grease; but not parts. There are about 150 contracts of this type. Again, regular monthly payments are made in fixed amounts.

The remaining 40 percent of sales is non-contract business involving individually negotiated engagements for major repairs and modernization.

The elevator maintenance service industry is described by the owner of the company as a "depression-proof" business affected very little by recessions or uncertain economic conditions. The demand for this service is stable and predictable. In addition to the contractual character of the business, repairs to elevators by their nature cannot be delayed and occur with some degree of regularity.

Within the industry there does exist some competition in the immediate market area which could affect the stability of this particular firm's sales. There are thirteen businesses offering similar services. The company is one of the largest of these. Although the demand for this type of service is highly predictable and inelastic, competition among firms is not hinged exclusively to price. Rather, non-price factors centering primarily on dependability and quality of service seem to be very important. The company appears to possess the needed combination of price and other factors as exhibited by continued profitability under the direction of its owner during the past eighteen years.

To complete the general profile of the company, its statements of financial position and operations for the fiscal year ending in May, 1967, are presented. These are the firm's actual statements prepared by an independent accounting firm. The Balance Sheet is shown in Figure 8. The Income Statement appears in Figures 9a and 9b.

Figure 8

THE COMPANY

BALANCE SHEET AS OF MAY 31, 1967

ASSETS

	Cost	*Accumulated Depreciation*	*Book Value*	
CURRENT ASSETS				
Petty Cash Fund				$ 100.00
Cash in Bank				68,311.21
Accounts Receivable				58,888.29
Advances				1,154.60
Work in Progress			$35,898.37	
Less: Advanced from Customers			29,470.56	6,427.81
Inventory of Supplies				52,631.87
Deposits				102.00
Total Current Assets				$187,615.78
FIXED ASSETS				
Buildings	$31,000.20	$ 7,767.97	$23,232.23	
Truck and Autos	18,794.92	10,475.00	8,319.92	
Furniture and Equipment	14,400.95	9,679.54	4,721.41	
Shop Equipment	8,590.90	6,245.24	2,345.66	
Building Improvements	17,938.72	5,277.76	12,660.96	
	$90,725.69	$39,445.51	$51,280.18	
Land			2,500.00	
Total Fixed Assets				53,780.18
OTHER ASSETS				
Cash Surrender Value of Officer's Life Insurance			$ 4,032.50	
Investment			111.75	
Prepaid Insurance			6,369.93	

Prepaid Interest		299.68	
Prepaid Taxes		298.08	
Total Other Assets			11,111.94
Total Assets			$252,507.90

LIABILITIES AND NET WORTH

CURRENT LIABILITIES			
Note Payable			$ 7,500.00
Note Payable–Auto			2,299.68
Accounts Payable			14,053.87
Accrued Use Tax Payable			189.48
Payroll Taxes Payable			4,382.98
Accrued Payroll Payable			20,897.66
Accrued Profit Sharing Contribution Payable			20,555.67
Accrued Expenses Payable			1,870.32
Note Payable–Insurance			5,538.33
Corporation Income Tax Payable–F.Y.E. 5/31/67			6,737.49
Customers' Deposits			5,594.53
Total Current Liabilities			$ 89,620.01
NET WORTH			
Capital Stock Issued		$ 10,000.00	
Retained Earnings–June 1, 1966	$133,197.79		
Net Profit for the Period	21,349.58		
Less: Officers' Life Insurance	(1,659.48)		
Total Retained Earnings		152,887.89	
Total Net Worth			162,887.89
Total Liabilities and Net Worth			$252,507.90

Figure 9a

THE COMPANY

STATEMENT OF INCOME AND EXPENSE

	Fiscal Year Ended May 31, 1966		*Fiscal Year Ended May 31, 1967*	
SALES–CONSTRUCTION	$ 75,063.75	100.0%	$	....
Less: Cost of Sales	63,804.81	85.0	.....	....
Gross Profit	$ 11,258.94	15.0%	.....	....
SALES–MODERNIZATION	$134,975.66	100.0%	$ 39,470.00	100.0%
Less: Cost of Sales	90,842.88	67.3	23,807.23	60.3
Gross Profit	$ 44,132.78	32.7%	$ 15,662.77	39.7%
SALES–SERVICE	$ 41,620.70	100.0%	$ 72,946.81	100.0%
Less: Cost of Sales	22,634.74	54.4	39,154.60	53.7
Gross Profit	$ 18,985.96	45.6%	$ 33,792.21	46.3%
SALES–REPAIRS	$152,784.34	100.0%	$220,297.28	100.0%
Less: Cost of Sales	87,300.45	57.1	122,783.19	55.7
Gross Profit	$ 65,483.89	42.9%	$ 97,514.09	44.3%
SALES–FULL MAINTENANCE	$231,756.58	100.0%	$268,763.66	100.0%
Less: Cost of Sales	111,696.61	48.2	128,974.69	48.0
Gross Profit	$120,059.97	51.8%	$139,788.97	52.0%

SALES–INSPECTION	Included in		$ 39,124.75	100.0%
Less: Cost of Sales	Sales-Service		21,203.11	54.2
Gross Profit	for 5/31/66		$ 17,921.64	45.8%
TOTAL SALES	$636,201.03	100.0%	$640,602.50	100.0%
Less: Total Cost of Sales	376,279.49	59.2	335,922.82	52.4
Gross Profit on Sales	$259,921.54	40.8%	$304,679.68	47.6%
OTHER INCOME				
Discounts Earned	$ 588.18	....	$ 898.64	....
Other Income	(148.37)	....	577.41	....
Total Other Income	$ 439.81	0.1%	$ 1,476.05	0.2%
TOTAL GROSS PROFIT	$260,361.35	40.9%	$306,155.73	47.8%
OPERATING EXPENSES (Schedule I)*	$222,414.03	34.9%	$257,239.56	40.2%
OPERATING PROFIT	$ 37,947.32	6.0%	$ 48,916.17	7.6%
EMPLOYEES PROFIT SHARING PLAN	9,619.60	1.5%	20,555.67	3.2%
NET PROFIT BEFORE TAXES	$ 28,327.72	4.5%	$ 28,360.50	4.4%
CORPORATION INCOME TAX PAYABLE	6,843.18	1.1%	7,010.92	1.1%
NET PROFIT FOR THE FISCAL YEAR	$ 21,484.54	3.4%	$ 21,349.58	3.3%

*See Figure 9b.

Figure 9b

THE COMPANY OPERATING EXPENSES

**Schedule I*

	Fiscal Year Ended May 31, 1966		*Fiscal Year Ended May 31, 1967*	
SHOP EXPENSES				
Depreciation	$ 7,220.82		$ 8,049.67	
Employee Training	1,773.19		2,923.42	
Foreman's Wages	13,700.67		13,828.35	
Free Maintenance	2,699.89		761.49	
Insurance	9,521.14		13,693.61	
Miscellaneous	180.07		105.01	
Shop Expenses	3,082.18		2,720.19	
Shop Wages	14,054.71		9,193.20	
Stand-By-Pay	333.71		1,805.04	
Unallocated Wages	9,919.49		12,480.03	
Taxes and Licenses	13,204.43		18,172.92	
Tool Expense	375.88		526.25	
Uniforms	1,061.89		1,327.49	
Welfare Ins. and Employee Benefits	8,178.63		11,271.19	
Total Shop Expenses	$ 85,306.70	13.4%	$ 96,857.86	15.1%
GENERAL AND ADMINISTRATIVE EXPENSES				
Advertising	$ 4,182.49		$ 5,985.22	
Audit and Legal	6,321.38		7,437.90	
Bad Debts	27.62		207.91	
Car and Truck Expense	5,024.37		5,554.08	
Donations	904.75		1,029.60	
Dues and Subscriptions	1,248.27		1,741.40	
Interest	660.99		944.37	
Light and Heat	1,574.96		1,704.87	
Maintenance	1,431.78		1,130.72	
Miscellaneous	154.15		181.47	
Office Expense	5,015.72		7,873.32	
Promotion and Travel	9,410.32		8,232.47	
Rent	344.00		168.00	
Telephone and Telegraph	5,937.80		7,336.21	
Wages–Office	45,738.13		52,500.16	
Wages–Officer	38,119.25		41,766.00	
Wages–Sales	11,011.35		16,588.00	
Total General and Administrative Expenses	$137,107.33	21.5%	$160,381.70	25.1%
Total Operating Expenses	$222,414.03	34.9%	$257,239.56	40.2%

The Present Exchange System

To begin analyzing the effect of the introduction of a centralized financial exchange system, a description of the company's present financial exchange activities and related costs will be presented. Currently, the exchange function is performed by four individuals who devote some portion of their time to the following activities requiring "out-of-pocket" expenditures:

– Monthly billing of contract holders and other receivables. This involves locating the customer's ledger card, addressing the invoice, and entering the amount of the billing. Computations leading to the amount to be billed for non-contract sales may be necessary. In a majority of cases, however, the invoice amount is the same each month based on contract agreements. Invoices are prepared during the first few days of each month. The terms are 30 days cash with no discount offered.

– Receiving and entering customers' payments. A large portion of remittances are received from the 15th to the 20th of each month. Many customers also wait the full 30 days before paying.

– Preparing and mailing bank deposits. This is done approximately 12 to 15 times per month. Checks are entered on a deposit form and mailed to the bank. Cash is seldom handled.

– Cash disbursements for accounts payable. Invoices are filed when received as to the due dates with discount. Payment is delayed as long as possible within the limits of the discount period. The net price of the invoice is computed and a check is written and mailed on the due date. Checks are signed by the company's treasurer. The pattern of disbursements during the month is described as "even" with no major peaks or dips. Only a small proportion of the invoices are discountable. These are generally paid on the 10th day of each month.

– Cash disbursements for payroll items. The company's forty employees are paid by check on Friday with a one week lag in payment. A separate checking account is maintained for the payroll account. Ten employees receive fixed salaries and thirty require hourly computations. Payroll tax contributions are paid quarterly as specified by the governmental bodies involved.

Bank Relations

The company's bank relations are described as informal and satisfactory. No service charges are incurred. Compensating balances are not formally required although the company has traditionally maintained a substantial amount in its account, which is apparently satisfactory from the bank's point of view.

An informal line of credit of $50,000 was established during 1967 and a term loan of $25,000 is currently outstanding. The note was discounted at a 6.5 percent rate of interest on an unsecured basis. The bank has requested that the firm maintain at least $50,000 in working capital. Financial statements have not been required by the bank.

Balance Sheet Accounts: Assets

The balance sheet classifications of the company are typical of traditional exchange systems and present concepts of liquidity. On the asset side of the balance sheet, several accounts are related to financial exchange.

Of primary importance is the cash account, whose function is exclusively that of liquidity for transactions purposes. In addition, other accounts are being used for exchange purposes and differ from the cash account only in so far as the timing of exchanges is concerned. The accounts receivable balance is one such account which contains approximately five weeks' sales which are continually outstanding. Presumably the reason for such an account is to facilitate operations by offering the convenience of delayed payment. Such a convenience has a cost to the firm and must be recovered.

Funds have also been committed to employee advances. Here the timing of exchanges is again reflected, since value has been paid out before services have been received. This represents a cost to the firm which must, in some way, be recovered, since interest is not charged explicitly for these loans.

The prepaid accounts for taxes and interest, too, carry time costs which should be recognized. These are financial items not related directly to production.

Finally, the implications of the account "advanced from customers" should be noted. Values in this account have been described as cash received for the completed portion of specified repair contracts in progress. In this case, there is a matching of services performed and value received so that time costs of exchange are not present. It therefore seems appropriate to reduce "work in progress" by the amount of customers' advances as has been done since the work has actually been performed. Only a contingent liability remains for the satisfactory completion of the total contract and such liabilities are not formally recognized in this company's accounts.

The financial exchange assets, then, consisting of cash, accounts receivable, employee advances, and prepayments must be assessed with the ongoing cost. Their purpose is to facilitate exchange. As such, they require financing and must therefore generate revenues sufficient to compensate these funds.

Sources

On the liability side of the company's balance sheet are reflected the sources of funds which are being used to finance the firm's total asset structure. It is the total composition and related cost of these funds which determine the earning rate required of assets. Each item has a cost. In combination, an average cost of capital arises.

Within the current payables of the company's balance sheet are located a variety of accounts traditionally associated with short-term liquidity. The timing of exchanges is reflected by these accounts. In general, real values have already been received by the company but settlement has been delayed. In most cases, no explicit interest charge is present. Accounts payable and accrued expenses payable are examples of such "free" sources of funds. Similarly, taxes payable and wages payable represent the controlling of funds with no explicit interest charge. Finally, the customers deposits account represents value "earned" and received on uncompleted contracts. This account might alternatively be described as an equity account falling in the category of long-term sources and related costs.

Considering these sources together, since they are being used by the company and fall within its control, costs should be recognized. With the introduction of the central exchange system, some of these costs may be eliminated and substituted with the bank interest rate for short-term credit.

Income Statement Accounts

The income statement of the company exhibits several accounts containing financial exchange items. These are bad debts, dues and subscriptions, interest, office expense, office wages, and discounts earned. With the exception of discounts earned, these accounts are associated with the handling of the firm's exchange function as described above. Discounts earned could alternatively be eliminated by subtracting this value from cost of sales thereby arriving at a figure closer to the "cash" price of the goods. It is when these discounts are lost that they become identifiable as an explicit financing charge.

Application of the Model

The application of the indifference model will be presented by following the sequence of factors identified in Chapter IV. As a factor is added, the required data will be presented followed by its *IXR* computation.

Factors I, I-A, II: Financial Assets

The cost of carrying financial assets is measured by applying the earning rate on investments required to compensate the various capital costs. Data must therefore be collected or computed for the company's investment in financial exchange assets and its cost of capital rate.

The approach used in this case study for the determination of the needed values was to rely on historical data. This approach assumes that historical data are representative of values expected in the future. It was felt that even with the possible shortcomings of this assumption, the resulting computations would be more valid than if purely subjective estimates of expected values were used.

The values used for the company's financial asset investment and cost of capital rate are based on average or normal figures drawn from actual operating data for twenty-four consecutive months. This period includes the completed fiscal years of 1965-1966, and 1966-1967. These average data appear to be more representative of the firm's behavior than do simple year-end balance sheet accounts. Thus the first step in the application was to construct normalized financial statements for the period selected. The data for the twenty-four months observed are presented in Table 3. A completed balance sheet incorporating these values is shown in Figure 10. This figure also exhibits the firm's normalized operating data using the averaged values for the two-year period.

Computation of the Cost of Capital

In the preceding discussion of sources of funds it was asserted that regardless of the source, all funds within the control of the firm are accompanied by costs. In some cases, such as notes payable, this cost is explicitly stated and is therefore readily identifiable. The costs of other sources, however, are not readily identifiable. They are hidden. Nonetheless, they are present and could be eliminated if the credit source itself were eliminated.

Figure 10

NORMALIZED FINANCIAL STATEMENTS

The Company
Normalized Balance Sheet

Financial Exchange Assets:		*Current Sources:*	
Petty Cash Fund	$ 100	Accounts Payable	$ 11,300
Cash in Bank	34,700	Expenses Payable	2,000
Cash–Payroll	5,500	Payroll Payable	9,100
Accounts Receivable	46,500	Use Tax Payable	....
Employee Advances	2,100	Payroll Tax Payable	4,700
Prepaid Taxes	700	Income Tax Payable	4,800
Prepaid Interest	700	Notes Payable	13,000
	$ 90,300		$ 44,900
Real Assets	$119,600	Other Sources	$165,000
	$209,900		$209,900

The Company
Normalized Income Statement

Sales		$638,400
Cost of Sales		355,350
Gross Profit		$283,050
Expenses:		
Shop	$ 91,000	
G & A	148,700	239,700
Net Income		43,350
Profit Sharing		15,000
Net Income Before Tax		28,350
Income Tax		6,950
Net Income		$21,400

Table 3

NORMALIZED ACCOUNTS

(*thousands of dollars*)

Month	*Petty Cash*	*Cash in Bank*	*Cash Payroll*	*Accounts Receivable*	*Employee Advances*	*Prepaid Taxes*	*Prepaid Interest*	*Accounts Payable*
1	.1	42.2	4.9	60.8	0.5	0.1	...	16.8
2	.2	54.1	5.4	56.2	2.6	0.7	1.0	21.2
3	.2	44.7	5.5	59.2	2.7	0.6	1.0	14.6
4	.2	56.8	7.3	47.0	2.7	0.4	0.9	16.8
5	.1	41.0	5.6	50.4	2.9	0.3	0.8	21.6
6	.1	46.0	5.6	60.1	2.9	0.1	0.8	18.4
7	.1	58.2	5.7	39.7	3.1	1.1	0.7	21.5
8	.1	54.0	5.9	42.9	3.2	0.9	0.8	14.4
9	.1	61.6	6.1	27.1	3.2	0.7	0.8	14.1
10	.1	55.4	6.2	42.5	3.2	0.6	0.7	14.1
11	.1	28.2	6.2	48.8	4.2	0.4	0.7	11.9
12	.1	43.2	6.2	36.3	...	0.3	0.5	5.1
13	.1	40.0	7.8	26.6	1.8	0.1	0.5	6.6
14	.1	16.7	7.5	47.1	1.7	7.6	6.0	10.2
15	.1	11.4	6.1	38.0	1.7	0.6	0.5	2.3
16	.1	21.8	4.5	44.9	1.6	0.5	0.5	1.2
17	.1	10.4	6.2	31.2	1.2	0.3	0.5	4.9
18	.1	14.2	7.7	40.8	1.7	0.1	0.4	7.1
19	.1	8.0	7.9	42.7	1.9	0.3	0.3	2.8
20	.1	5.1	...	53.9	1.8	1.0	0.3	2.0
21	.1	5.6	7.9	57.7	1.7	0.8	0.2	1.1
22	.1	23.0	7.9	49.8	1.7	0.6	0.1	20.0
23	.1	24.0	...	54.6	2.1	0.5	0.1	9.8
24	.1	68.3	...	58.9	1.2	0.3	0.3	14.1
Avg. Bal.	.1	34.7	5.5	46.5	2.1	0.7	0.7	11.3

Month	*Expenses Payable*	*Payroll Payable*	*Accrued Use Tax*	*Accrued Payroll Tax*	*Accrued Income Tax*	*Note Payable Insurance*	*Note Payable Bank*	*Note Payable Auto*
1	0.8	6.3	...	6.7	7.7	...	...	...
2	3.7	5.9	...	5.0	6.6	14.3	...	...
3	2.9	7.5	...	4.1	6.1	14.3	...	...
4	2.7	4.5	...	4.6	6.5	14.3	...	...
5	0.5	7.1	0.1	4.0	6.2	13.9	...	...
6	0.5	8.1	0.1	4.2	3.7	13.3	...	...
7	1.1	8.1	0.3	4.2	2.6	12.6	...	...
8	...	8.7	0.1	5.2	2.7	12.1	...	...
9	0.1	9.1	0.2	6.0	3.0	11.4	...	...
10	...	14.3	0.1	6.8	3.4	10.7	...	...
11	0.1	9.8	...	6.1	15.5	10.1	...	...
12	9.9	18.0	...	4.9	5.6	9.7	...	...
13	17.3	11.5	...	3.3	6.6	9.3	...	...
14	2.7	19.4	...	2.6	6.6	14.0	...	...
15	0.1	8.0	0.1	6.4	3.3	13.6	...	...
16	0.2	9.4	...	5.9	3.6	13.8	...	...
17	0.1	5.0	0.2	3.1	3.3	11.8	...	...
18	0.8	6.8	...	3.8	0.7	12.3	7.5	...
19	2.4	5.9	...	5.2	1.8	9.8	7.5	...
20	2.1	6.8	...	1.3	2.4	8.9	7.5	...
21	...	7.8	...	5.1	4.4	7.9	7.5	...
22	0.1	4.2	0.5	7.4	3.2	7.0	7.5	...
23	0.1	7.1	0.1	3.1	3.5	7.1	7.5	...
24	1.9	20.6	0.2	4.4	6.7	5.5	7.5	2.3
Avg. Bal.	2.0	9.1	0.0	4.7	4.8	Avg. Bal. of combined notes payable 13.0		

To compute the company's cost of capital, each source of funds will be imputed with a cost at a level which is thought to satisfy its most likely alternative earning opportunity. For example, wages payable, were they in the possession of the employee, could be invested at an interest rate from time deposits with no apparent change in risk. Similarly, other sources may be imputed with such rates. Each source will be discussed separately and an average cost of capital rate will be computed.

Accounts and expenses payable. Short-term credit supplied by other firms carries with it the lending firm's average cost of capital rate. If immediate cash settlement is not realized, then the lending firm must forgo investment opportunities in its primary activity and apply funds within its control to the exchange function to create accounts receivable. Hence, from its point of view, a before-tax amount of revenue must be recovered to meet these earning requirements. Although it is impossible to identify precisely the amount of this rate, it can be approximated. Using an average figure for the cost of capital of industrial firms, an 8 percent after tax rate has been identified.[1] Applying an average effective corporate tax rate of 40 percent,[2] an approximation of the before-tax financial exchange charge for credit to the holder of accounts payable is 13 percent.

Payroll payable. The opportunity investment rate for pending wages is approximated by the before-tax return on time deposits which is near 4 percent.

Taxes payable. This source of funds is virtually riskless from the viewpoint of the lender—the government. The pure interest rate may therefore be used in this case as an approximation of the related time cost. The pure interest rate ranges near 5 percent.

Notes payable. The cost of notes payable of the company can be measured by relating the average amount borrowed to the interest expense paid. The average amount borrowed for the period studied has been determined as $13,000. Interest expense for the same period averages $780 per year. This represents a before-tax cost of 6 percent.

Equity. Finally, the cost of equity capital must be estimated. Since this is a closely held company with no established market value, a subjective measurement of the cost of equity must suffice. This approach relies on the opinion of the owner concerning the level of earnings of the firm related to his investment. The opinion was expressed that current levels of earnings are satisfactory. It was further stated that if funds were readily available, they could be reinvested at current levels of profitability. These levels of profitability are expected to continue into the relevant period of future operations. These statements may be used to support the measurement of this firm's equity capital and alternative investment opportunities as reported earnings divided by equity. Using this rationale, the cost of equity capital is approximately 13 percent.

The tax rate. To compute the firm's cost of capital using the method selected, the effective corporate income tax rate is needed. This figure is obtained by dividing the average taxable income for the period being studied by the average tax paid. An effective tax rate of 24.5 percent results for this firm.

The average cost of capital. By combining these costs of the individual sources of funds and averaging them by their proportional amount in the capital structure, a measure of the firm's cost of capital is obtained. The computation appears as follows:

Source	*Amount ($)*	*Proportion (%)*	*Cost After Tax (%)*	*Index*
Accounts and Expenses Payable	13,300	6.3	13 × 75 = 9.75	61.40
Payroll Payable	9,100	4.2	4 × 75 = 3.00	12.60
Taxes Payable	9,500	4.6	5 × 75 = 3.75	17.25
Notes Payable	13,000	6.3	6 × 75 = 4.50	28.35
Equity	165,000	78.6	13.00	1,021.80
		100.0%		1,141.40

1,141.4 ÷ 100% = 11.4%, the average cost of capital.

Sales. The sales for the two years studied were $636,201 for 1965, and $640,602 for 1966. Accordingly, an average figure of $638,400 will be used in the analysis.

Computation of the IXR for Financial Assets

To begin the computation of indifference rates, information is now in usable form for the first group of factors concerning the cost of maintaining assets for financial exchange. These assets include petty cash, cash in bank, cash–payroll, accounts receivable, employee advances, prepaid interest, and prepaid taxes. The indifference rate for these factors will be labeled as IXR_{fa} and is computed as:

$$IXR_{fa} = \frac{1}{S}\left[\frac{AFA \times CC}{(1 - TR)}\right]$$

where: IXR_{fa} = Indifference Exchange Rate for Financial Assets
AFA = Average Financial Assets
CC = Cost of Capital
TR = Tax Rate

$$IXR_{fa} = \frac{1}{\$638{,}400}\left[\frac{\$90{,}300 \times .114}{(1 - .245)}\right]$$

$$IXR_{fa} = 2.13\%.$$

Factors III and IV: Variable Exchange Costs and Variable Credit Costs

The variable costs incurred by the firm for the exchange function appear in the "General and Administrative Expenses" section of the schedule of operating expenses. The relevant accounts are Office Expense, Office Wages, Bad Debts, and Dues and Subscriptions. For the exchange activities described earlier in this chapter, it was estimated by the president of the company that one full-time or equivalent employee could assume the fragments now performed by four employees. The value of the services of this employee have been estimated at $10,000 per year.

Concerning office expenses for supplies and other costs related to the exchange function, an estimate of 25 percent of the total expense is so attributed resulting in a figure of $1,600 per year. Of this, approximately $450 represents collection fees paid to an accounts receivable collection agency. The remainder is for materials such as checks, postage, invoices, and working papers.

Finally, $125 is recognized as an average figure for bad debts and subscription fees for a credit rating service.

The total variable costs for exchange and credit activities are reflected as $11,725 per year. The indifference rate transformation appears as follows:

$$IXR_{vc} = \frac{VC}{S}$$

where: IXR_{vc} = Indifference Exchange Rate—variable costs of exchange and credit
VC = Total variable costs for exchange and credit

$$IXR_{vc} = \frac{\$11{,}725}{\$638{,}400}$$

$$IXR_{vc} = 1.83\% .$$

Factor V: Payables

As discussed in Chapter IV, the adoption of the central exchange system enables the firm to release its financial exchange assets for alternative uses. Accompanying this release of funds is the removal of an equal amount of sources of funds. Each source—short term and long term—is shrunk proportionally thus leaving the debt:equity ratio unaffected. Present short-term liabilities are liquidated with funds secured from the central exchange system so that the current liabilities are owing exclusively to the central system in the form of bank credit payable.

In this case study, \$90,300 in financial exchange assets are removed from the firm's asset structure. Accordingly, \$90,300 are also removed from the source structure. This results in a new level of total sources of capital of \$119,600 comprised of 79 percent or \$94,000 in equity, and 21 percent or \$25,600 in short-term bank credit. The bank credit interest rate is assumed to be equal to the present average cost of short-term sources which is 7.4 percent. An average cost of capital showing the new levels of obligations may now be computed as follows illustrating the fact that the average cost of capital remains unchanged.

Source	*Amount*	*Proportion (%)*	*Cost After Tax (%)*	*Index*
Bank Credit	25,600	21.4	7.4 × 75 = 5.6	119.8
Equity	94,000	78.6	13.0	1,021.8
		100.0		1,141.6

1,141.6 ÷ 100% = 11.4%, the average cost of capital.

If the theoretical costs of the several categories of payables are eliminated as the central system is adopted, and the bank's interest rate is substituted for these costs, then the indifference rate is not affected. The question therefore arises for this company in particular as to whether or not such price decreases will be realized. As a practical matter, it is unlikely that wages would be changed or that taxes would be reduced to separate out the time costs associated with these liabilities. Reductions in cost in these areas would probably not be realized.

There is also some doubt about receiving cash prices from suppliers for purchases. However, it has been indicated by present banking spokesmen that companies will have to offer "cash discounts" if the system is to be effective. There is likely, therefore, to be pressure in the direction of offering cash prices. Accordingly, this reduction will be assumed in the study.

Finally, the one item of cost which can be said with certainty will be eliminated is the interest expense on notes payable. Since the borrowing itself will be eliminated, the interest will be avoided.

To include the effect of the substitution of bank credit for current sources of short-term funds, a comparison is necessary between the theoretical cost reductions due, and the actual reductions expected.

Source	*Amount*	*Rate*	*Theoretical Reduction*	*Actual Reduction*
Accounts and Expenses Payable	$13,300	13%	$1,730	$1,730
Payroll Payable	9,100	4	365	0
Taxes Payable	9,500	5	475	0
Notes Payable	13,000	6	780	780
			$3,350	$2,510

Theoretical Reductions in Cost	=	$ 3,350
Actual Reductions Expected	=	−2,510
Net Increase in Cost (J)		$ 840

By incurring this additional cost, the indifference exchange rate must be reduced if the firm's total financial position is to remain unaffected. This factor is expressed as:

$$IXR_{bc} = \frac{-J}{S}$$

where: IXR_{bc} = Indifference Exchange Rate—short-term bank credit
$-J$ = Net additional cost of substituting bank credit for present sources of funds

$$IXR_{bc} = \frac{-\$840}{\$638{,}400}$$

$$IXR_{bc} = -.13\% .$$

Factor VI: Profit

This variable includes two items which could cause the firm's profit figure to change as a result of adopting the centralized system of exchange. First, the possibility of a change in the quantity of services demanded should be considered. Would the shifting of the credit function from the firm to the central system cause a gain or loss in the company's unit sales? The opinion has been expressed by the owner of the company that the credit aspect of the business is not a marketing tool used to obtain sales. Credit is extended by tradition for 30 days "cash terms" with no discount offered for more rapid payment. The 30 days cash terms are extended simply to accommodate the routine of the purchasers' accounting and settlement systems. Such a period allows payment to be made within a "billing" cycle, which is normal for the present methods of financial exchange. It therefore appears that the use of alternative credit sources would have no effect on the quantity of services sold by this firm. No unit sales would be gained or lost.

The second consideration brought about by the shifting of the credit function to the banking system is the elimination of the time costs of carrying the receivables. Again, a cash price for the goods can be offered thereby reducing selling prices. This price advantage would then be redirected to the banking system if credit is to be used by the purchaser. As was suggested in the discussion of the cost of accounts payable, such price reductions are likely to be a normal part of the centralized system. To recognize this reduction, the following computation is suggested by the model:

$$\frac{AR \times CC}{(1 - TR)} = \frac{\$46{,}500 \times .114}{.755} = \$7{,}070.$$

By reducing revenue by the amount of $7,070, net income after taxes is reduced by $5,340. The loss of this profit must be converted to an indifference factor on a before-tax basis and subtracted from the total rate thus far determined.

$$IXR_k = \frac{K}{S}$$

where: IXR_k = Indifference Exchange Rate—revenue adjustments
K = Change in Revenue

$$IXR_k = \frac{-\$7,070}{\$638,400}$$

$$IXR_k = -1.11.$$

Factor VII: Revenue Changes and the Exchange Rate Computation

The exchange rate thus far determined must be modified to accommodate the change in revenue associated with Factor VI. This modification is computed as follows:

$$IXR' = \frac{S}{S_e} \times IXR_s$$

where: S = Unadjusted Sales
S_e = Adjusted Sales
IXR_s = The unadjusted indifference exchange rate
IXR' = The adjusted indifference exchange rate

$$\frac{S}{S_e} = \frac{\$638,400}{\$638,400 - 7,070}$$

$$\frac{S}{S_e} = 1.01.$$

Summary of the Applied Model

The complete indifference exchange rate model was expressed in Chapter IV as:

$$IXR' = \frac{1}{S_e}\left[\frac{CC(ACB + MS + AR)}{(1 - TR)} + VEC + VCC - II + J + K\right]$$

where: IXR' = Indifference Bank Exchange Rate
ACB = Average Cash Balance
MS = Marketable Securities
CC = Cost of Capital

VEC = Variable Exchange Costs
VCC = Variable Credit Costs
II = Interest Income
TR = Tax Rate
J = Net savings or net cost of changing from trade credit to bank credit
K = Gain or loss of profit due to change in unit sales or change in selling price per unit
S = Unadjusted Sales
S_e = Sales adjusted for expected changes in K.

In the application of the model, more suitable notations were substituted for the original items as follows:

AFA = Average Financial Assets including the original variables of ACB, MS, and AR. Other financial assets are also included in this variable. These are Petty Cash, Employee Advances Receivable, and Prepaid Taxes and Prepaid Interest
VC = Variable costs including VEC and VCC
II = Interest Income was eliminated in this case study since the firm has no marketable securities or accompanying interest.

These modifications result in the following expression of the model as it was applied in the study:

$$IXR' = \frac{1}{S_e}\left[\frac{CC(AFA)}{(1-TR)} + VC + J + K\right].$$

The application of the data collected in the case study may be summarized to reflect the following values for the variables and the total indifference exchange rate computation:

AFA = \$90,300
CC = 11.4%
VC = 11,725
TR = 24.5%
J = −840
K = −7,070
S = 638,400
S_e = 631,330

$$IXR' = \frac{1}{\$631{,}330}\left[\frac{.114 \times \$90{,}300}{.755} + \$11{,}725 - \$840 - \$7{,}030\right]$$

$$IXR' = 2.75\% .$$

This same rate was obtained as the individual factors were introduced as:

$$\begin{aligned} IXR_{afa} &= 2.13\% \\ IXR_{vc} &= 1.83 \\ IXR_{bc} &= -.13 \\ IXR_{k} &= -1.11 \\ IXR &= 2.72 \\ \frac{S}{S_e} &= \times 1.01 \\ IXR &= 2.75\%. \end{aligned}$$

Figure 11

FINANCIAL STATEMENTS REFLECTING CENTRAL EXCHANGE SYSTEM

Balance Sheet

Real Assets	$119,600	Bank Credit	$ 25,600
		Equity	94,000
	$119,600		$119,600

Income Statement

			adjustment*
Sales		$631,330	(1) $7,070
Cost of Sales		353,620	(2) 1,730
Gross Profit		277,710	
Expenses:			
Shop Expenses	$ 91,000		
General and Adm.	136,195		(3) 10,000
Total		227,195	(3) 1,600
		50,515	(3) 125
Bank Exchange Service Exp.		17,445	(3) 780
		33,070	
Profit Sharing		15,000	
Net Operating Income		18,070	
Bank Interest Expense		1,910	
Net Income Before Tax		16,160	
Income Tax		3,960	
Net Income		$12,200	

*These adjustments are keyed to the cost comparisons appearing on the following page.

Financial Statements: Recast

If the centralized system were adopted for this company at the specified indifference exchange rate, the statements shown in Figure 11 would result.

Cost Comparisons.

*adjustment	Item	Computation	Amount
	Present System:		
	Average Financial Assets	$90,300 × .114 =	$10,290
	Reduction in Payables	$44,900 − 25,600 × .056 =	−1,080
			9,210
(2)	Purchase Price Reductions	$ 1,730	
(3)	Wages Expense	10,000	
(3)	Supplies Expense–Office	1,600	
(3)	Bad Debts	125	
(3)	Interest Expense	780	
		$14,235 × .755 =	10,740
	Total Eliminated Costs		$19,950
	Eliminated Revenue:		
(1)	Selling Price Reductions	$ 7,070 × .755 =	−5,340
	Total Cost		$14,610
	Central System:		
	Bank Exchange Service Expense	$17,445 × .755 =	$13,170
	Bank Interest Expense	1,910 × .755 =	1,440
	Total Cost		$14,610

Benefits and Limitations of the Application: Conclusion

It has been the purpose of this case study to apply the indifference model and concepts underlying an integrated financial exchange system to a practical business situation in order to gauge their potentials and limitations. Several observations and conclusions have resulted from this investigation.

Specifically, it may be concluded that for the company studied, a rate of 2.75 percent of sales has been identified as the expenditure level required to equate total costs under both the present exchange system and the system of central exchange. Thus the conclusion may be reached that any rate less than 2.75 percent will lead to economies for the firm. It is the ability to specify this rate which has been the primary purpose of this study.

Although it is believed that the cost relationships posed by the indifference model are valid, and a rate has been specified which exhibits a degree of apparent accuracy, reservations persist. Limitations resulting from restricting assumptions and measurement difficulties cannot be overlooked even in the face of the numerical symmetry of the indifference model. In the last analysis, the ability to measure the input variables must again be exposed for consideration. In this case study, historical values representing a two-year period were used as proxies for expectations of future values. It was felt that these actual values, considering their limitations, were nonetheless more reliable than purely subjective estimates of the ideal, but elusive, expected values. This limitation should therefore be recognized when evaluating the results of the case study.

The use of an "average" cost of capital rate also poses limitations. This method was used because its computation rests on data which are relatively objective. More sophisticated cost of capital measurement techniques such as the marginal cost approach may be theoretically superior but lack the objectivity of the method used. Since the concept of the cost of capital is, in itself, controversial almost to the point of being arbitrary, it is felt that the method used in the study does not severely limit its validity.

To the contrary, it is in the application of the cost of capital consideration, itself, which is significant. Even in the face of imprecision, this case study has added credence to the concept of the opportunity costs associated with financial exchange assets. In discussing the approach of the model with the personnel of the company studied, in addition to interviews with individuals occupying similar positions in other companies, the point was established that cash balances and other financial exchange assets carry substantial costs for the company in the performance of its exchange function. It was generally agreed by the several individuals participating in this study that many continuing costs of financial exchange are left unrecognized when considering the cash and credit functions as they are conducted at present. By applying the model, these costs are identified and may be acknowledged as a part of the total cost of financial exchange. It is this total cost currently being incurred which serves as a basis for evaluating the efficiencies and economies thought to be offered by a centralized exchange system.

Finally, the problem of liquidity risk must be considered. The question arises as to the ultimate effect of the removal of cash balances and other liquid assets on the firm's liquidity. By eliminating these assets, is the total risk of the firm increased? Does the firm's capitalization rate increase to reflect added risk? Is the firm insolvent? It is hoped that the answer to these questions is now apparent. It is precisely this risk which the centralized system will assume in return for the exchange service fee. The model poses the method which can measure the amount the firm can pay for liquidity services. It remains for the banking system to determine the feasibility of accepting the responsibility for facilitating exchange within the cost limits of the indifference exchange rate.

VII
Summary and Conclusions

The prospect of the checkless society is expected to present to the firm and the economy the opportunity to increase the efficiency of exchanges of value leading to added returns for the suppliers of capital. This development would be consistent with the objectives of profit maximization. In this study, the description of such an exchange system, its observable development to date, and a method for evaluating its effect on the firm have been presented. It is the purpose of this final chapter to summarize the results of the study and to consider their implications. A question will also be raised concerning the non-economic consequences of the new system and possible negative ramifications.

The Checkless Society and the Firm's Liquidity

The principal benefit of the integrated financial exchange system is expected to lie in its ability to relieve the firm of many of the repetitive actions and related costs which are necessary to support the firm's liquidity and facilitate exchange. These items are concerned with the processing of receipts and disbursements of cash, the functions related to credit operations, and the costs associated with the continued investment in financial current assets. All of these costs are incurred for the purpose of allowing the firm to interact with other producing-consuming units, thus enabling it to pursue its specialized productive activity at an optimal rate. The processes of exchange permit the firm to gain access to demanders of its production value, to identify and verify the propriety of value being offered in exchange, and to execute or record the exchange.

The ability of the integrated financial exchange system utilizing automated equipment to bring further efficiency to the processes of exchange will permit the specializing firms to further intensify their productive efforts thus leading to an increased individual and total product. The communication network of the exchange system will allow for instant transfers of value thus releasing float and temporarily idle balances for alternative investment at a minimal cost. Centralized stores of information on the firm's ability to generate value added in its primary productive activity will fulfill the exchange requisite of identifying and verifying value. This will release cash balances for investment in other functions and allow the economy to reach new levels of credit with no added risk. Duplicated efforts for traditional credit investigation and evaluation will be eliminated. Finally, the centralized records and the network will allow exchanges of value to be executed and recorded electronically, thus eliminating the need for manual or machine handling at the firm and replacing postage and personnel requirements.

Liquidity, or the ability to interact with other firms and exchange value, will therefore assume a new interpretation. This interpretation returns to the firm's primary reason for being—the generation of value added. So long as the firm continues to demonstrate that it is efficient in its primary activity with a continuous growth in value, there should be no question of its ability to secure resources for operations needed to continue this growth. In its central position with instantly retrievable data on the firm's ability to add value, the bank will facilitate the exchange function by performing the needed services.

The benefits of the centralized exchange system are not, however, without cost. To establish the system, a capital investment must be made by the banking system for the computer network facility. Funds will also be needed for its continued operation. To compensate the system for its services and cover these costs, the firm will be assessed a variable expense which is likely to be geared to the discounting of sales. If the system is to reach efficient levels, the total cost of the central system as measured by the sum of the fees charged to businesses must be less than the total costs being incurred at present under traditional practices.

Whereas the individual firm is now faced with the decision as to the level of investment required to facilitate its exchange needs based on current procedures, a large part of this decision and the accompanying risks will be passed to the centralized system. In doing so, the firm will rid itself of many of the effects of fixed cost-volume-profit movements stemming from investments in the exchange function and obtain a new flexibility in these activities. Exchange costs become variable and fluctuate directly with changes in demand. The firm's risk therefore filters back to the fixed costs associated with the investment in its primary activity. Again, the extent to which the firm is able to continue this production efficiently is the key to its ability to participate successfully in the centralized exchange system. Value added results in continued access to the services of exchange.

The Indifference Exchange Rate Model

The primary purpose of this study has been to develop a method for determining the cost implications to the firm of the concepts which underlie the checkless society. The development of such a method is viewed as a first step toward the implementation of the proposed system of exchange, since it offers a means for measuring the resources which would be available to establish the new system. In essence, for a firm to view the new system favorably, it must be demonstrated that an equivalent quality of service can be provided by the system at a cost which is no more than the cost now being incurred using traditional methods. This cost as measured by the method developed in this study is expressed as an indifference bank exchange rate.

The indifference bank exchange rate model is essentially a marginal analysis approach to the problem which poses the identification of costs which would be avoidable by the firm due to the introduction of the new system. Once isolated, these costs are then transformed and expressed in terms of the probable compensation method to be used by the banking system—a discounting of sales revenues. Thus the indifference bank exchange rate represents the amount of expense that the firm could absorb to offset exactly the various costs which the new system would eliminate.

If the economies offered by the automated equipment of the central system materialize as they have been forecast, then the actual bank exchange rate charged to the firm will be less than the indifference rate, and the firm will thereby achieve economies and higher levels of efficiency.

As presented in Chapter VI, for the single firm which has been studied, an indifference rate of 2.75 percent of sales was determined. If the banking system can service the exchange needs of this firm for an actual rate which is lower than the 2.75 percent indifference rate, economies will be realized.

Suggested Further Research

In this study the relationships which have been identified and discussed remain extremely distant from the point where they could be implemented with a predictable degree of accuracy. Further research is required if implementation is to be prudently approached. This research appears to be in two areas which depend largely upon each other. First, a more precise statement must be developed concerning the exact services which the banking system can offer to the firm. This must consider macroeconomic effects and the ability of the system to control economic activity under the new concepts of exchange.

Second, given a more precise statement of the services which the central system could offer with the macroeconomic constraints, a more accurate application of the indifference exchange rate model would be possible. By applying the model to a large number of heterogeneous firms, the feasibility of implementing the total system or parts of it could be analyzed with increased certainty. The method of analysis presented in this study should serve as a basis for this further study.

Limitations of the Model

There are two principal limitations to the effectiveness of the method of analysis offered in this study. First, there exists the difficulty of quantifying several of the variables which have been identified. Second, a question must be raised concerning the validity of the profit maximization objective.

Regarding the measurement of variables, lack of precision is especially encountered when attempting to quantify the firm's cost of capital rate and also the effect on the firm's sales resulting from the removal of credit extension from its control. The cost of capital rate must, at best, be an approximation. There is no way to measure it precisely, since it rests largely on expectations and evaluations of risk and uncertainty. Nonetheless, the broader concept itself is valid and must be recognized in light of its imprecision. This problem of uncertainty is not new. It is present in most business decisions. To refuse to cope with problems of uncertainty or to exclude the imprecise variables from the analysis would be more damaging than to handle such problems and face the inherent risks. The cost of capital variable in the indifference model is one such item.

Similarly, the variable representing the effect on sales associated with the shifting of the credit function from the firm to the bank also poses measurement difficulties. Again, such uncertainty must be gauged by knowledgeable individuals prepared to assume the risks of business management. Empirical research designed to relieve this uncertainty would seem to be equally difficult since, quite obviously, no historical data can exist on a development which has not yet occurred.

The other principal limitation of the method of analysis and the validity of its measurements concerns the profit maximization assumption. It is the discussion of this limitation which is presented in the following concluding paragraphs.

Implications of the Checkless Society

From the point of view of profit maximization, if the banking system can offer to the firm the exchange service at a rate which is lower than its indifference rate, the new system should be accepted. Returns to capital suppliers would increase. Yet there remains the question as to the ultimate desirability of such an objective. Such increased returns may, in fact, be at the greater expense of non-economic, non-profit maximization variables which the indifference model does not consider. This possibility must be recognized in the final analysis of the problem's implications.

The Benefit of Added Information

From the firm's point of view, the centralized exchange system will provide added information concerning the use of its operating and long-term resources. In its exchange account with the central system will be recorded the inflows and outflows of value resulting from operating transactions. If this account continually exhibits an average balance of zero, then the firm reflects an efficient, non-aggressive policy for the use of short-term or operating funds. It has succeeded in causing its inflows and outflows of value for operating items to coincide over a relatively short period of time at the exchange expense cost assessed by the banking system. As the coincidence of inflows and outflows is increased, the efficiency of the transfer mechanism rises to the ultimate point where all resources are invested continually and idle balances do not exist. Only the exchange fee remains.

Alternatively, if the exchange account exhibits an average balance which is negative, then a more aggressive policy is reflected by the use of short-term resources. To determine the desirability of a policy of maintaining a negative balance, financial leverage effects must be considered. In general, a firm which is efficient in its primary activity can favorably employ this short-term borrowing relationship to improve its overall returns. Such a relationship would be expected of the "normal" or "model" firm participating in the system.

It is the other extreme situation in which the centralized system most revealingly demonstrates its information-producing capability. Here the exchange account continually exhibits a positive average balance which is likely to reflect a non-aggressive, non-maximizing management attitude. The resources in the firm's exchange account are within its realm of responsibility for efficient usage. Yet they continue to earn only minimal returns as paid by the banking system. Since, by definition, the firm's objective is to be efficient in a specialized activity, returns from the continued investment in the banking system as reflected by a positive balance are not appropriate. These funds should be invested in the firm's primary activity or returned to the capital suppliers for alternative investment or consumption.

The centralized financial exchange system as applied to the firm, then, serves as an information source which is capable of identifying inefficiency in the use of short-term funds used by the production sector of the economy. Non-maximizing firms are identified. If, in fact, the objective of the economy is the maximum efficiency in the use of these capital resources, then the management of firms exhibiting non-maximizing characteristics such as the accumulation of enormous cash and near cash balances should be adjusted, or their scale of operations should be reduced. In the central exchange system, such firms would build up positive balances in their exchange accounts and therefore be identified as non-maximizers. A producing firm does not have this prerogative of "saving" as would be exhibited by continuing positive balances. This prerogative is reserved for other sectors of the economy whose values are other than productive efficiency in the economic sense.

The Cost of Efficiency in Exchange: Conclusion

If profit maximization can be accepted as a valid measure of the society's aim, then the exchange system suggested by the concepts of the checkless society and automatic credit and money transfer systems appears to present a means for moving closer to that aim. The indifference model will measure potential gains of such a movement. As a result, emphasis will be increased on the efficiency with which a product or service is performed and financed. A clear distinction will be realized between the "cash price" of the product or service and the financing charges related to this output. The explicit financing charges and accompanying risks can be evaluated to determine the total efficiency of the firm.

This new information capability, founded deeply in concepts of time values and opportunity costs, will eliminate such practices as "free" trade credit extended to inefficient, marginal accounts. The fact will be recognized that there is a continuing cost related to this credit which may be hidden in selling prices, costs of goods sold, deteriorating liquidity ratios which remain unacknowledged, or forgone opportunities. Idle liquidity resulting from a firm's inability to apply it to profitable uses will also be rectified.

The ability to measure accurately a firm's performance by relating value added to financing costs will permit a more precise evaluation of the efficiency with which such value added actually is generated. The result of this increased capability will be the elimination of inefficiency and the maximum return to capital investment. From the point of view of the profit maximization assumption, this elimination will benefit the economy.

Yet the profit maximization assumption itself needs to be questioned. If values other than those included in the narrow objective of profit maximization should dominate, then many of the supposed benefits of an integrated financial exchange system do, in fact, assume the character of costs and not benefits. Further specialization is continually encouraged under the centralized system. Economies gained by massive scale operations are sought out. The development of generalized, non-economic values and activities is thwarted. Individuals who are unable to attain the levels of efficiency demanded by the system are forced to drop out. Social costs rise.

The question of the desirability of the complete acceptance of the profit maximization directive which has led to the concepts of the checkless society therefore appears to become relevant. This is a difficult question. Its answer is elusive. Yet it must be pondered when the giant step reflected by the investment required by a system of fully computerized financial exchange is under consideration. Specialization in exchange can generate benefits. It also can destroy values.

Notes

CHAPTER I

1. Dale L. Reistad, "Implications of Checkless Banking Systems" (address at the Third Annual Meeting of the Joint Sessions of the Midwest Business Administration Association and Midwest Economics Association, April 21, 1967), p. 14.
2. J. M. Keynes, *The General Theory of Employment, Interest, and Money* (New York: Harcourt, Brace & Co., 1936), p. 170.
3. J. C. Burton, "The Management of Corporate Liquid Assets" (unpublished Ph.D. dissertation, Columbia University, 1962), p. 125.
4. John Newell McKinney, "Corporate Liquidity in the Postwar Period" (unpublished Ph.D. dissertation, University of California, 1965).
5. "News and Ideas," *Burroughs Clearing House*, April, 1967, p. 16.
6. W. Putman Livingston, "Virtues of the Checkless Society: Good for the Public, Good for Banks," *The American Banker*, June 14, 1967, p. 4.
7. George W. Mitchell, "Effects of Automation on the Structure and Functioning of Banking" (remarks at the Annual Meeting of the American Economic Association, New York City, December 28, 1965), p. 3.
8. *Ibid.*, p. 5.
9. A. W. D. Cox and H. M. Zeidler, *A Techno-Economic Study of Methods of Improving the Payments Mechanism* (Stanford, California: Stanford Research Institute, December, 1966).
10. John J. Clarke, "Hard Figures and Considered Judgments on Progress Towards the Checkless Society," *The American Banker*, February 17, 1967.
11. Diebold Group, *Summary Report of a Survey on the Impact of Electronics on Money and Credit* (New York: The Diebold Research Program, 1967), question #27, p. 19.
12. G. W. Mitchell, *op. cit.*, p. 5.

CHAPTER II

1. W. P. Livingston, "Virtues of the Checkless Society: Good for the Public, Good for the Banks," *American Banker*, June 14, 1967, p. 4.
2. *Ibid.*, p. 4.
3. Rupert J. Ederer, *The Evolution of Money* (Washington, D. C.: Public Affairs Press, 1964), p. 7.

4. *Ibid.*, p. 16.
5. George W. Mitchell, "Tomorrow's Money as Seen Today" (remarks at the Annual Stockholders Meeting of the Federal Reserve Bank of Boston, October 6, 1966), p. 1.

CHAPTER III

1. Peter H. Burgher, "Comment of a New Cash Receipts Technique," *The Arthur Young Journal,* April, 1957, p. 19.
2. *Ibid.*, p. 20.
3. Sidney M. Robbins, "Getting More Mileage Out of Cash," *N.A.A. Bulletin,* September, 1960, p. 68.
4. Christine Pinches, "Lock Box Banking–Key to Faster Collections," *Credit and Financial Management,* June, 1967, p. 16.
5. *Ibid.*, p. 18.
6. "Money at Work," *The Wall Street Journal,* August 29, 1961, p. 1.
7. "Making Cash Work Overtime," *Business Week,* July 12, 1958, p. 121.
8. "Money at Work," *op. cit.*, p. 1.
9. *Ibid.*, p. 14.
10. *Ibid.*, p. 14.
11. "Chicago Clearing House Clearing Freight Bills," *Burroughs Clearing House,* February, 1966, p. 10.
12. *Ibid.*, p. 10.
13. John Sagan, "A Theory of Working Capital Management," *The Journal of Finance,* May, 1955, p. 125.
14. J. C. Burton, "The Management of Corporate Liquid Assets" (unpublished Ph.D. dissertation, Columbia University, 1962), p. 41.
15. "Stretching the Cash: Firms Get Along Well on Very Little Money," *The Wall Street Journal,* October 7, 1966, p. 12.
16. Benjamin H. Beckhart, *Business Loans of American Commercial Banks* (New York: The Ronald Press, 1959), p. 139.
17. "Stretching the Cash: Firms Get Along Well on Very Little Money," *The Wall Street Journal,* October 7, 1966, p. 12.
18. *Ibid.*, p. 12.
19. James P. Furniss and Paul S. Nadler, "Should Banks Reprice Corporate Services?" *Harvard Business Review,* May-June, 1966, p. 96.
20. *Ibid.*, p. 100.
21. *Ibid.*, p. 103.
22. Ed. Tying, "Compensating Balances: Are They on the Way Out?" *Burroughs Clearing House,* July, 1967, p. 34.
23. Christine Pinches, *op. cit.*, p. 26.
24. Robert H. Cole, *Financing Retail Credit Sales Through Charge Account Bank Plans,* Business Management Survey, No. 5 (Bureau of Business Management, College of Commerce and Business Administration, University of Illinois, Urbana, Illinois), p. 8.
25. *Ibid.*, p. 8; W. F. Hofmann, "The Experience of Industrial Trust and Savings Banks in the Field of Charge Account Banking" (unpublished Ph.D. dissertation, Ball State Teachers College, Muncie, Indiana, 1959), p. 4; and Harlan R. Patterson, "A Study of Charge Account Banking and Its Financial Performance" (unpublished Ph.D. dissertation, Michigan State University, 1963), p. 15. Patterson also notes the "Buy-O-Matic" plan of R. A. Doussear developed in 1941.

26. "Charge-It with the Bank," *Business Week,* September 23, 1950, p. 58.
27. Patterson, *op. cit.,* p. 16.
28. Sidney P. Allen, "A Credit Card Operation That's Hit the Jackpot," *Burroughs Clearing House,* September, 1964, p. 51.
29. Sidney P. Allen, *op. cit.,* p. 103.
30. Patterson, *op. cit.,* p. 22; and Hofmann, *op. cit.,* p. 6.
31. "Chase Manhattan to Sell Credit Card Business for About $9 Million," *The Wall Street Journal,* January 31, 1962, p. 8.
32. "Throwing in the Sponge," *Forbes,* February 1, 1962, p. 15.
33. "Bank Americard Sales Zoom," *Burroughs Clearing House,* February, 1969, p. 18.
34. Allen, *op. cit.,* p. 51.
35. "Bank Credit Cards and the Law," *The Bankers Magazine,* Winter, 1969, p. 36.
36. "Charge-It with the Bank," *op. cit.,* p. 58.
37. Cole, *op. cit.,* p. 38.
38. Hofmann, *op. cit.,* p. 7.
39. Patterson, *op. cit.,* p. 77.
40. Allen, *op. cit.,* p. 103.
41. "Bank Credit Card Expansion," *Bankers Monthly Magazine,* June 15, 1966, p. 44.
42. "News and Ideas," *op. cit.,* January, 1967, p. 16.
43. *Ibid.,* p. 15.
44. *Ibid.,* April, 1967, p. 16.
45. George W. Mitchell, "Effects of Automation on the Structure and Functioning of Banking," *op. cit.,* p. 2.
46. John J. Clarke, "Hard Figures and Considered Judgments on Progress Towards Checkless Society," *The American Banker,* February 17, 1967.
47. B. Cox, *et al.,* SRI Project 6154, December, 1966.
48. John J. Clarke, *op. cit.,* p. 5.
49. W. Putman Livingston, "Virtues of the Checkless Society: Good for the Public, Good for Banks," *The American Banker,* June 14, 1967, p. 4.
50. "Taking 'Blue Sky' Out of 'Checkless Banking,'" *Burroughs Clearing House,* April, 1967, p. 35.
51. W. Putman Livingston, *op. cit.,* p. 4.
52. *Ibid.*
53. Richard E. Sprague, "A System for Automatic Value Exchange," *The Quarterly,* June, 1967, p. 2.
54. James V. Vergari, "The Credit Card–Input to the Checkless Society," Federal Reserve Bank of Philadelphia, May, 1967.
55. Lawrence A. Welsch, "A Proposal to Automate Money," *Business Topics,* Autumn, 1966, p. 59.
56. Melvin E. Salveson, "A New Medium of Exchange," *Banking,* December, 1966, p. 99.
57. George W. Mitchell, "Fed Prepares for Evolving Money Transfer Systems," *American Banker,* December 1, 1966, p. 1A.
58. "Taking 'Blue Sky' Out of 'Checkless Banking,'" *op. cit.,* p. 75.
59. *Ibid.*
60. "Three Groups Study Payments 'Mechanisms,'" *Burroughs Clearing House,* October, 1966, p. 19.
61. William Zimmerman, "Banks in Three Areas Contemplating Pilot Checkless Societies," *American Banker,* July 10, 1967.

62. William Zimmerman, "Pa., Ohio Banks Greet Checkless Society with Direct Utility Bill Debit," *American Banker,* June 29, 1967, p. 1.
63. "Hempstead Banks 'Black Box' Demonstration Gets Enthusiastic Response from Merchants," *American Banker,* January 13, 1967, p. 2.
64. Livingston, *op. cit.,* p. 4.
65. John F. Elsbree, "Credit Aspects of Total Automation," *Burroughs Clearing House,* June, 1966, p. 37.
66. George W. Mitchell, "Effects of Automation on the Structure and Functioning of Banking," *op. cit.,* p. 4.
67. "Taking 'Blue Sky' Out of 'Checkless Banking,'" *op. cit.,* p. 75.

CHAPTER V

1. David B. Hertz, "Risk Analysis in Capital Investment," *Harvard Business Review,* January-February, 1964, p. 99.
2. Robert Schlaifer, *Introduction to Statistics for Business Decisions* (New York: McGraw-Hill Book Company, Inc., 1961), pp. 16-17.
3. This procedure is developed in the Hertz article.
4. The application of probabilities as presented herein uses *discrete* values in the computation. These discrete values act as estimates or averages of *continuous* probability distributions which may also be used if a more statistically precise result is desired. The nature of the immediate problem lends itself more readily to the estimated, discrete approach as described.
5. It should be noted that this multiplication rule for determining the probability of an *IXR* must be modified if the variables are *dependent* upon each other. This modification will be illustrated later in the sample problem to be presented.
6. In reality this tax rate may be effectively less than 50 percent. Further, the certainty of the rate may be less than 1.00. Again, these figures are used for illustrative purposes.
7. Since the tax rate has an assumed probability of occurrence of 1.0, it will have no effect on the total probability and may therefore be eliminated.

CHAPTER VI

1. J. F. Weston and E. F. Brigham, *Managerial Finance* (2d ed.; New York: Holt, Rinehart and Winston, 1966), p. 306.
2. U.S. Bureau of the Census, Statistical Affairs, *Statistical Abstract of the United States,* "Corporation Income Tax Returns Summary, 1940-1964," p. 403.

Bibliography

Books and Monographs

Beckhart, Benjamin H. *Business Loans of American Commercial Banks*. New York: The Ronald Press, 1959.

Cole, Robert H. *Financing Retail Credit Sales Through Charge Account Bank Plans*. Business Management Survey, No. 5. Urbana, Illinois: Bureau of Business Management, College of Commerce and Business Administration, University of Illinois, 1955.

Cox, B., Dana, A. W., and Zeidler, H. M. *A Techno-Economic Study of Methods of Improving the Payments Mechanism*. Prepared for the Subcommittee on Improving the Payments Mechanism—The Federal Reserve System by the Stanford Research Institute, Menlo Park, California, SRI Project 6154, December, 1966.

Diebold Group. *Summary Report of a Survey on the Impact of Electronics on Money and Credit*. The Diebold Group, Inc., 1967.

Ederer, Rupert J. *The Evolution of Money*. Washington, D. C.: Public Affairs Press, 1964.

Federal Reserve Bank of Boston. *Electronic Money . . . and the Payments Mechanism*. Annual Report, 1967.

Keynes, J. M. *The General Theory of Employment, Interest, and Money*. New York: Harcourt, Brace & Co., 1936.

"Managing Company Cash," *Studies in Business Policy*, #99. New York: National Industrial Conference Board, 1961.

Schlaifer, Robert. *Introduction to Statistics for Business Decisions*. New York: McGraw-Hill Book Company, 1961.

Smith, Paul. *The Cost of Providing Consumer Credit*. National Bureau of Economic Research, Occasional Paper 83, 1962.

The Association for Bank Audit, Control and Operation. *An Electronic Network for Check Collection, A Feasibility Study*. Park Ridge, Illinois: NABAC, 1966.

U.S. Bureau of the Census, Statistical Affairs. *Statistical Abstract of the United States.* Washington, D. C.: Government Printing Office, 1967.

Weston, J. F., and Brigham, E. F. *Managerial Finance.* 2d ed. New York: Holt, Rinehart and Winston, 1966.

Articles

"ABA, Fed Will Assist New NABAC Project." *The American Banker,* November 22, 1966.

Abouchar, Roger J., Magnis, Nicholas E. "Bank Credit Cards—Implications for the Future." *Bankers Monthly Magazine,* January 15, 1967, p. 22.

Agemian, Charles A. "Credit Card Avalanche: Risks High Enough as It Is, Let's Not Compound Them by Hiding the Real Issues." *The American Banker,* March 21, 1967.

Allen, Sidney P. "A Credit Card Operation That's Hit the Jackpot." *Burroughs Clearing House,* September, 1964, p. 50.

"American Bankers Association National Automation Conference, New York." *Banking,* April, 1965, p. 108.

Anthony, R. N. "The Trouble with Profit Maximization." *Harvard Business Review,* November-December, 1960, p. 134.

"Bank Americard Sales Zoom." *Burroughs Clearing House,* February, 1969, p. 18.

"Bank Credit Cards and the Law." *The Bankers Magazine,* Winter, 1969, p. 36.

"Bank Credit Card Expansion." *Bankers Monthly Magazine,* June 15, 1966, p. 44.

"Bank Credit Cards Gaining Popularity." *Financial World,* January 4, 1961, p. 7.

"Bargain Day at the Money Store." *American Banker,* June 15, 1967.

Baumol, W. J. "Marginalism and the Demand for Cash in Light of Operations Research Experience." *Review of Economics and Statistics,* August, 1958, p. 209.

______. "The Transactions Demand for Cash: An Inventory Theoretic Approach." *Quarterly Journal of Economics,* November, 1952, p. 545.

"Boundary Jumping—Electronic Style." *Forbes,* September 15, 1966, p. 39.

Brooke, Phillip. "Retailers Asked to Study Checkless Payments." *American Banker,* January 12, 1968, p. 1.

"Build-Up in Cash." *Fortune,* July, 1964, p. 90.

Burgher, Peter H. "Comment on a New Cash Receipts Technique." *The Arthur Young Journal,* April, 1957, p. 19.

Butt, Ralph E. "Designing a Central File to Meet Tomorrow's Needs." *Banking,* March, 1967, p. 95.

"Buy Now, Pay Later." *Chain Store Age,* February, 1968, p. 30.

Camp, Charles B. "Slow Payers, More Firms Conserve Cash by Letting Bills Go Until Due—or Later." *Wall Street Journal,* October 7, 1966, p. 1.

Carroll, J. P. "Determining Computer Service Operating Costs." *Banking,* July, 1964, p. 42.

Cary, A. K. "Our Moneyless Society." *Burroughs Clearing House,* March, 1966, p. 43.

Carter, Norman H. "A Different View of the Checkless Society." *Banking,* February, 1967, p. 119.

Catt, A. J. L. "Idle Balances and the Motives for Liquidity." *Oxford Economic Papers,* June, 1962, p. 124.

"Charge-It at the Bank." *Business Week,* October 29, 1966, p. 104.

"Charge-It with the Bank." *Business Week,* September 23, 1950, p. 58.

"Chase Manhattan to Sell Credit Card Business for About $9 Million." *The Wall Street Journal,* January 31, 1962, p. 8.

"Checkless Society Check." *Banking,* May, 1967, p. 115.

"Chicago Clearing House Clearing Freight Bills." *Burroughs Clearing House,* February, 1966, p. 10.

Clarke, John J. "Better Payments Must Offer Benefits to Consumers, Retailers." *American Banker,* January 15, 1968, p. 5.

______. "Check-Out Time for Checks." *The Business Lawyer,* July, 1966, p. 931.

______. "Hard Figures and Considered Judgments on Progress Towards Checkless Society." *American Banker,* February 17, 1967, p. 5.

Corey, Roger M. "An Individual Bank Study of the Checkless Society." Worcester County Bank, Worcester, Massachusetts, May, 1967.

______. "'Checkless' Society? Bank Working on How, When and Why." *American Banker,* December 1, 1966, p. 1A.

"Credit Card Is Studied by 5 New York Banks." *Wall Street Journal,* March 22, 1967, p. 8, col. 2.

Cross, John J. "How We Put Commercial Loans 'On-Line.'" *Banking,* May, 1966, p. 39.

"Discipline, Control and Direction." *American Banker,* July 11, 1967.

Duesenberry, J. S. "The Portfolio Approach to the Demand for Money and Other Assets." *Review of Economics and Statistics,* February, 1963, p. 9.

Duncan, James H. C., Sikes, Jr., Allen B. "Charge-Account Banking Has Made the Grade." *Bankers Monthly,* November 15, 1957, p. 42.

"Electronic Cashless Society Developments May Basically Change Monetry Structure." *Credit and Financial Management,* May, 1967, p. 13.

"Electronic Money." *Forbes,* April 1, 1967, p. 42.

"Electronic Payment System 'Inevitable.'" *American Banker,* February 16, 1967, p. 3.

Elsbree, John F. "Credit Aspects of Total Automation." *Burrough's Clearing House,* June, 1966, p. 37.

"Enlarging the Charge-Card." *Business Week,* May 28, 1966, p. 42.

"Federal Reserve Board Studies Credit Cards." *Wall Street Journal,* March 2, 1967, p. 12, col. 4.

Feinstein, Marvin C. "The Checkless Society." *Bank Equipment News,* April, 1967, p. 14.

Fox, R. Gerald. "Trends in Bank Systems & Equipment Design." *Bankers Monthly Magazine,* May 15, 1966, p. 38.

"FNB of Nev. Introduces Master Charge Plan; Commerce Union Offers All-Purpose Card." *American Banker,* January 16, 1968.

Furniss, James P., and Nadler, Paul S. "Should Banks Reprice Corporate Services?" *Harvard Business Review,* May-June, 1966, p. 95.

Gilliland, J. C. "Centralized Credit . . . One Clearing House." *The Credit World,* September, 1963, p. 15.

"Governor Mitchell Considers Tomorrow's Banking." *Banking,* December, 1966, p. 33.

Groome, James J. "Preauthorized Payments." *Burroughs Clearing House,* March, 1968, p. 28.

Hammerton, James. "Is the Consumer Ready for 'Checkless Society?'" *Bankers Monthly Magazine,* November 15, 1967, p. 37.

"Hempstead Banks 'Black Box' Demonstration Gets Enthusiastic Response from Merchants." *American Banker,* January 13, 1967, p. 2.

Hertz, David B. "Risk Analysis in Capital Investment." *Harvard Business Review,* January-February, 1964, p. 95.

"Industrial NB Plans Credit Card; FN, Atlanta, to Offer Bank Americard." *American Banker,* January 11, 1968, p. 1.

"Interbank Card Discussing Interchange Plan in Europe." *American Banker,* February 1, 1968, p. 1.

"Interbank Card Sets U.S. Interchange by November 1." *American Banker,* October 18, 1967, p. 1.

"Impact of Electronics on Money and Credit." *Bankers Monthly Magazine,* April 15, 1967, p. 56.

Johnson, J. E. "Bank Automation: A Look at the Next 5 Years." *Bankers Monthly,* December, 1964, p. 44.

Johnson, Robert W. "Basic Trends in Consumer Credit." *Credit Currents,* April, 1965, p. 16.

Karr, Albert R. "Stretching the Cash." *Wall Street Journal,* October 6, 1966, p. 1.

Kramer, R. L., and Livingston, W. P. "Cashing in on the Checkless Society." *Harvard Business Review,* September-October, 1967, p. 14.

Lanzillotti, R. "Pricing Objectives in Large Companies." *The American Economic Review,* December, 1958, p. 921.

Lee, Norris F. "What's This 'Checkless Society' All About?" *Financial Executive,* June, 1967, p. 18.

Livingston, W. P. "Banking's Role Cited in Development of Financial Information Utility." *American Banker,* December 1, 1966, p. 7A.

______. "Banking's Role in Credit Card Economy." *Banking,* September, 1966, p. 111.

______. "Stage Being Set for New System, 'Electro-Terms' Translate Concepts." *American Banker,* December 1, 1967.

______. "Why Return the Checks." *The Bankers Magazine,* Summer, 1966, p. 15.

______. "Virtues of the Checkless Society: Good for the Public, Good for the Banks." *American Banker,* June 14, 1967, p. 4.

Long, Robert H. "System Improvement, Not Check Elimination, Key to Efficient Transmission of Funds." *Bankers Monthly Magazine,* June 15, 1967, p. 50.

Magnis, Jr., Nicholas E., and Pickell, Barry. "Credit Card Banking." *Bankers Monthly Magazine,* November 15, 1966, p. 31.

"Major Obstacles Seen to National Computer System." *American Banker,* June 6, 1967.

"Making Cash Work Overtime." *Business Week,* July 12, 1958, p. 121.

Manger, Charles C. "Yardstick for Cost of Investment in Accounts Receivable." *Credit and Financial Management,* June, 1967, p. 24.

Mathews, Richard S. "Checkless Society Is Inevitable; Banks Must Prepare for It Now." *The American Banker,* May 6, 1966.

______. "The Role of Other Industries in a Checkless Society." New York: Booz, Allen & Hamilton, Inc., May, 1967.

Milburn, William G. "Automated Customer Services: Problems & Potentials." *Bankers Monthly Magazine,* May 15, 1966, p. 32.

Mitchell, George W. "Automation and Banking Structure." Remarks at the American Institute of Banking, Philadelphia Chapter, Forum, March 8, 1967.

______. "Confrontation Within Banking: Machines vs. Bankers or Bankers With Machines," June 6, 1966.

______. "Effects of Automation on the Structure and Functioning of Banking." Remarks at the annual meeting of the American Economic Association, New York City, December 28, 1965. Published in *The Journal of Accountancy,* March, 1966, p. 60.

______. "Fed Prepares for Evolving Money Transfer System." *American Banker,* December 1, 1966, p. 1A.

______. Statement before the Legal and Monetary Affairs Subcommittee of the Committee on Government Operations, House of Representatives, February 9, 1966.

———. "Tomorrow's Money as Seen Today." Remarks at the Annual Stockholders Meeting of the Federal Reserve Bank of Boston, October 6, 1966.

"Money Goes Electronic in the 1970's." *Business Week,* Special report, January 13, 1968, p. 54.

"NABAC Study Shows Electronic Check Collection System Is Feasible." *The American Banker,* November 22, 1966.

Nadler, Paul S. "Checkless Society: Don't Wait Until It Comes to Face Up to It." *The American Banker,* October 26, 1966.

"New Look at Cash." *Fortune,* August, 1965, p. 96.

"News and Ideas." *Burroughs Clearing House,* April, 1967, p. 16.

"News and Ideas." *Burroughs Clearing House,* January, 1967, p. 15.

O'Connor, R. Emmett. "From a Pioneer: Tips on Credit Card Operation." *Burrough's Clearing House,* April, 1967, p. 38.

Odlin, R. "Automation Expands Functions of Banks." *Office,* January, 1965, p. 79.

Patterson, Harlan R. "A Study of the Markets Served by Bank Charge Plans." *The Credit World,* October, 1964, p. 13.

Pechman, H. "Instant Cash for Your Company." *Credit & Financial Management,* July, 1964, p. 14.

Pinches, Christine. "Lock Box Banking—Key to Faster Collections." *Credit and Financial Management,* June, 1967, p. 16.

"People Have the Last Word in Electronic Money Society." *American Banker,* February 2, 1968, p. 5.

"Problems in Creating Checkless Society and Centralized Data Bases Discussed." *American Banker,* April 2, 1967.

Reinhardt, Hedwig. "Economics of Mercantile Credit: Its Place Among Nonfinancial and Financial Intermediaries." *Credit and Financial Management,* May, 1967, p. 24.

Reistad, D. L. "Automation's Trail to Tomorrow." *Banking,* June, 1965, p. 115.

———. "Banking Automation—1975." *Banking,* July, 1964, p. 45.

———. "Banks Should Lead Development of Preauthorized Payments Systems." *American Banker,* January 26, 1968, p. 5.

———. "Curtain Going Up: Presenting Automated Bank of Tomorrow." *The American Banker,* October 26, 1966.

———. "Implications of Checkless Banking Systems." Speech at the Third Annual Meeting of Midwest Economics Association, Chicago, Illinois, April 21, 1967.

———. "Ten Years of Revolution." *Banking,* August, 1965, p. 107.

———. "What Telecommunications Will Do for Banking." *Banking,* December, 1965, p. 108.

Robbins, Sidney M. "Getting More Mileage Out of Cash." *N.A.A. Bulletin,* September, 1960, p. 65.

Sagan, John. "A Theory of Working Capital Management." *The Journal of Finance,* May, 1955, p. 121.

Salveson, Melvin E. "A New Medium of Exchange." *Banking,* December, 1966, p. 99.

Schecter, Donald. "Cashless Society Is Not Science Fiction." *The American Banker,* October 24, 1966.

"Slow Payers, More Firms Conserve Cash by Letting Bills Go Until Due—or Later." *Wall Street Journal,* October 7, 1966, p. 1.

Sprague, Richard E. "A System for Automatic Value Exchange." *The Quarterly,* June, 1966, p. 2.

"Stepping Stones to the Checkless Society." *Burrough's Clearing House,* June, 1967, p. 23.

Stickney, George F. "Much Research Necessary Before 'Checkless' Society Can Become a Reality." *The American Banker,* December 7, 1966.

Stillman, R. N. "Short-Term Investment of Short-Term Cash." *Controller,* October, 1959, p. 455.

"Stretching the Cash." *Wall Street Journal,* October 6, 1966, p. 1.

"Taking 'Blue Sky' Out of 'Checkless Banking.'" *Burroughs Clearing House,* April, 1967, p. 35.

"The Checkless Society." *Bankers Monthly Magazine,* June 15, 1967, p. 30.

"The Computer and Credit Information." *Burroughs Clearing House,* January, 1968, p. 3.

"The Fifth National Automation Conference." *Banking,* June, 1967, p. 103.

"The Great Debate." *Burroughs Clearing House,* May, 1967, p. 17.

"Three Groups Study Payments 'Mechanism.'" *Burroughs Clearing House,* October, 1966, p. 19.

"Throwing in the Sponge." *Forbes,* February 1, 1962, p. 15.

Tobin, J. "Liquidity Preference as Behavior Towards Risk." *Review of Economic Studies,* February, 1958, p. 65.

Tying, Ed. "An Added Dimension in Financial Services." *Burroughs Clearing House,* July, 1965, p. 31.

———. "Compensating Balances: Are They on the Way Out?" *Burroughs Clearing House,* July, 1967, p. 34.

Vanderwicken, Peter. "Money at Work." *Wall Street Journal,* August 29, 1961, p. 1.

Vergari, James V., and McCarthy, John. "Centralized Data Bank Scrutinized." *The American Banker,* October 8, 1966.

Vergari, James V. "The Credit Card—Input to the Checkless Society?" Federal Reserve Bank of Philadelphia, Philadelphia, Pennsylvania, May, 1967.

———. "Obstacles Must Be Overcome on Way to Checkless Society." *The American Banker,* June 17, 1966.

Watterson, Lynn. "Checkless Agribanking—A Service of the Future." *Banking,* March, 1968, p. 95.

———. "Data Banks Can Protect Privacy." *Banking,* January, 1968, p. 56.

Welsch, Lawrence A. "A Proposal to Automate Money." *Business Topics,* Autumn, 1966, p. 59.

Westrup, W. H., and House, B. C. "Needed: A Central Source for Consumer Credit Data." *Burroughs Clearing House,* December, 1966, p. 33.

Whalen, Edward L. "A Cross-Section Study of Business Demand for Cash." *Journal of Finance,* September, 1965, p. 423.

"Workshop on Preauthorized Payment Plans Scheduled." *Banking,* January, 1968, p. 92.

Zimmerman, William. "Banks in Three Areas Contemplating Pilot Checkless Societies." *American Banker,* July 10, 1967.

———. "Consumer Education Called Major Task of Banks Effecting Checkless Society." *American Banker,* May 29, 1967, p. 1.

———. "Pa., Ohio Banks Greet Checkless Society with Direct Utility Bill Debit." *American Banker,* June 29, 1967, p. 1.

———. "Widespread Usage of 'Money Card' Seen." *American Banker,* February 16, 1967, p. 3.

Theses

Burton, John Campbell. "The Management of Corporate Liquid Assets." Columbia University, 1962.

Hofmann, W. F. "The Experience of Industrial Trust and Savings Banks in the Field of Charge Account Banking." Ball State Teachers College, Muncie, Indiana, 1959.

McKinney, John Newell. "Corporate Liquidity in the Post-War Period." University of California, Berkeley, 1965.

Patterson, Harlan Ray. "A Study of Charge Account Banking and Its Financial Performance." Michigan State University, 1963.

Skousen, Karl M. "Adaptability of Electronic Procedures to Bank Data Processing." Michigan State University, 1962.

PUBLICATIONS OF THE DIVISION OF RESEARCH

BUREAU OF BUSINESS AND ECONOMIC RESEARCH

MSU Business Studies

ELECTRONICS IN BUSINESS
Gardner M. Jones

ELEMENTARY MATHEMATICS OF LINEAR PROGRAMMING AND GAME THEORY
Edward G. Bennion

EXPLORATIONS IN RETAILING
Stanley C. Hollander

MARGINAL ASPECTS OF MANAGEMENT PRACTICES
Frederic N. Firestone

HISTORY OF PUBLIC ACCOUNTING IN THE UNITED STATES
James Don Edwards

CONTRIBUTIONS OF FOUR ACCOUNTING PIONEERS
James Don Edwards
Roland F. Salmonson

LIFE INSURANCE COMPANIES IN THE CAPITAL MARKET
Andrew F. Brimmer

BUSINESS CONSULTANTS AND CLIENTS
Stanley C. Hollander

THE AUTOMOTIVE CAREER OF RANSOM E. OLDS
Glenn A. Niemeyer

ELECTRONIC COMPUTATION OF HUMAN DIETS
Victor E. Smith

INTERNATIONAL ENTERPRISE IN A DEVELOPING ECONOMY
Claude McMillan, Jr., Richard F. Gonzalez with Leo G. Erickson

THE ENTERPRISING MAN
Orvis F. Collins, David G. Moore with Darab B. Unwalla

AGRICULTURAL MARKET ANALYSIS
Vernon L. Sorenson, editor

LABOR MARKET INSTITUTIONS AND WAGES IN THE LODGING INDUSTRY
John P. Henderson

THE EXECUTIVE IN CRISIS
Eugene Emerson Jennings

BANKING STRUCTURE IN MICHIGAN: 1945-1963
Robert F. Lanzillotti

RETAIL DECENTRALIZATION
Eli P. Cox and Leo G. Erickson

BANK ADMINISTERED POOLED EQUITY FUNDS FOR EMPLOYEE BENEFIT PLANS
Frank L. Voorheis

THE PERFORMANCE POST AUDIT IN STATE GOVERNMENT
Lennis M. Knighton

PASSENGER TRANSPORTATION
Stanley C. Hollander

THE EFFECTS OF DATA-PROCESSING SERVICE BUREAUS ON THE PRACTICE OF PUBLIC ACCOUNTING
Constantine Konstans

A SELECTED AND ANNOTATED BIBLIOGRAPHY ON SHOPPING CENTER MANAGEMENT
Bernard J. La Londe
Paul E. Smith

WORK ROLE INVOLVEMENT OF INDUSTRIAL SUPERVISORS
John G. Maurer

SELECTION OF NEW SUPPLIERS BY THE MOBILE FAMILY
James E. Bell, Jr.

THE CHECKLESS SOCIETY: ITS COST IMPLICATIONS FOR THE FIRM
William H. Mateer

INSTITUTE FOR INTERNATIONAL BUSINESS AND ECONOMIC DEVELOPMENT STUDIES

MSU International Business and Economic Studies

MICHIGAN'S COMMERCE AND COMMERCIAL POLICY STUDY
John L. Hazard

INTERNATIONAL DIMENSIONS IN BUSINESS
Recent Readings from BUSINESS TOPICS

MANAGEMENT DEVELOPMENT AND EDUCATION IN THE SOVIET UNION
Barry M. Richman

THE UNITED STATES OVERSEAS EXECUTIVE:
HIS ORIENTATIONS AND CAREER PATTERNS
Richard F. Gonzalez and Anant R. Negandhi

STEEL AND ECONOMIC DEVELOPMENT: CAPITAL-OUTPUT RATIOS IN THREE LATIN AMERICAN STEEL PLANTS
David G. Greene

ALTERNATIVE COMMERCIAL POLICIES – THEIR EFFECT ON THE AMERICAN ECONOMY
Mordechai E. Kreinin

INSTITUTION BUILDING IN BUSINESS ADMINISTRATION – THE BRAZILIAN EXPERIENCE
Donald A. Taylor

THE OPTIMAL STAGING AND PHASING OF MULTI-PRODUCT CAPACITY
Harold H. Wein and V. P. Sreedharan

EDUCATION FOR BUSINESS IN A DEVELOPING SOCIETY
Amar N. Agarwala

INSTITUTE OF PUBLIC UTILITIES

MSU Public Utilities Studies

DEVELOPMENT OF SEPARATIONS PRINCIPLES IN THE TELEPHONE INDUSTRY
Richard Gabel

MID-CONTINENT AREA POWER PLANNERS
W. Stewart Nelson

PERFORMANCE UNDER REGULATION
Harry M. Trebing, editor

RATE OF RETURN UNDER REGULATION: NEW DIRECTIONS AND PERSPECTIVES
Harry M. Trebing and R. Hayden Howard, editors

Public Utilities Papers

SELECTED STRUCTURE AND ALLOCATION PROBLEMS IN THE REGULATED INDUSTRIES
Manley R. Irwin and Milton Russell